Pathways to Integrity

Pathways to Integrity

ETHICS AND PSYCHOLOGICAL TYPE

BLAKE BURLESON

FOREWORD BY JOHN BEEBE

Published by
Center for Applications of Psychological Type, Inc.
2815 NW 13th Street, Suite 401
Gainesville, FL 32609
(352) 375-0160
www.capt.org

CAPT, the CAPT logo, and Center for Applications of Psychological Type are trademarks of the Center for Applications of Psychological Type, Inc., Gainesville, FL.

Myers-Briggs Type Indicator® and MBTI® are registered trademarks of Consulting Psychologists Press, Inc., Palo Alto, CA.

Introduction to Type™ is a registered trademark of Consulting Psychologists Press, Inc., Palo Alto, CA.

Printed in the United States of America.

ISBN 0-935652-64-7

Library of Congress Cataloging-in-Publications Data

Burleson, Blake Wiley.
Pathways to integrity: ethics and psychological type/
Blake W. Burleson; foreword by John Beebe.
     p. cm.
   Includes bibliographical references and index.
   ISBN 0-935652-64-7
   1. Typology (Psychology) 2. Ethics. 3. Jungian psychology.
   I. Title.
   BF698.3 .B86 2001
   170'.1'9—dc21

                                          2001032377

FOR HARRY WILMER

Contents

Foreword

This is a book that explores ideas that in my own work I have found to be essential. Chief among these conceptions, which might be called the first principles of a Jungian moral psychology, are the following: (1) that our ethical perspectives are necessarily grounded in our individual natures, (2) that Jung's typology helps to capture those individual particularities, (3) that the various types of psychological intelligence that Jung described in his 1921 book as "functions of consciousness" can be developed like so many muscle groups, and (4) that we must balance the strengths of the different functions if we are to develop their potential to make us more conscious and therefore more ethical. That potential, as Blake Burleson understands, goes beyond the narcissistic gentrification of our native typology into a real differentiation of our individual capacities to take care of others. Those who are already familiar with my work will find that Professor Burleson has emphasized many of the philosophical sources I hold dear, from Cicero to I. N. Marshall. The uses to which he puts the conceptual tools I have collected and sharpened, however, is very much his own. Blake Burleson wants us to see that there is more than one way to be ethical, indeed that there is even a typology of integrity itself. With his appealing directness, and the practical athleticism of his examples, he has developed a user-friendly guide to the different approaches that, in the game of life, people actually take when trying to meet their responsibility to others while remaining true to themselves. I can only be grateful that he shares my conviction that Jung's theory of typical functions of consciousness carries the seed of a truly psychological moral theory. That seed can now be certainly said to have germinated, in the process demonstrating the fertility of this field of inquiry as a ground for the study of integrity.

— JOHN BEEBE

Acknowledgments

I am grateful to Harry Wilmer, Jungian analyst and director emeritus of the Institute for the Humanities at Salado, for introducing me to the practical and personal side of Jungian psychology. He has inspired and given shape to a number of my projects.

I would like to thank John Beebe, Jungian analyst and Clinical Assistant Professor in Psychiatry at the University of California in San Francisco, for writing the foreword to the book. I believe that his work *Integrity in Depth*, along with Neumann's *Depth Psychology and a New Ethic* and Stein's *Solar Conscience/ Lunar Conscience*, represent the most important Jungian contributions to the field of ethics.

I recognize the members of Society for the Friends of Jung in Waco for their support and encouragement as I developed this project. I am also in debt to graduate students at Baylor University for allowing me to test these theories on them and for providing important support and correction to my ideas. Julie Burleson, my sister-in-law, took my photograph for the cover. Finally, I would like to thank the editorial staff at the Center for Applications of Psychological Type, especially Keven Ward, and Gordon Lawrence, author and teacher, who provided important suggestions, which made this a better book.

Chapter One

**AND WHY DO YOU NOT JUDGE FOR
YOURSELVES WHAT IS RIGHT?**

— JESUS OF NAZARETH

Introduction to Typology:
A Tool for Moral Decision Making

Judging for Ourselves

I once had a conversation with my six-year-old daughter that went like this. "Evan," I asked, "why is it wrong to hit someone?" She said, "Because they might hit you back." When I asked the same question to my son Garrett, who was nine at the time, he responded, "Because you could get caught and sent to the principal's office." My wife Sandy and I have taught our children some basic rules of right and wrong that I'm happy to say they usually follow, but their consistency in following the rules does not necessarily make them moral. Children can do the right thing without knowing why they ought to do the right thing. Yet to be morally mature we must know why our actions are right or why our actions are wrong. Being conscious of why we follow certain moral injunctions is as important as following them.

In our complex world, where we face ambiguous decisions every day, the task of moral decision making is not easy. To be confident of the decisions we make, we must know why we make them. As adults this knowledge cannot be based on someone else's moral authority, e.g., "My parents told me not to hit anybody." In order to decide for ourselves what is right, we must know for ourselves.

Thus, knowledge of self is an essential component of moral decision making. Pathways to Integrity explores morality from this starting point. Based on C. G. Jung's theories of psychological type as made practical through the Myers-Briggs Type Indicator (MBTI) personality inventory, this book aims to assist the reader in gaining insight into how our approach to moral decision making is based on our psychological type. This typological approach to ethics underscores self-knowledge as the foundation for our ability to judge for ourselves what is right.

The Type Theory of C. G. Jung

C. G. Jung (1885–1961) was a Swiss psychologist who studied with Sigmund Freud, the founder of modern psychology. The branch of psychology Jung founded is known as Analytical Psychology. This psychology places emphasis upon the role of the unconscious in the development of the individual. One of Jung's most important contributions to Western culture was his theory of psychological type. Words commonly used in our vocabulary today such as "introversion" and "extraversion" were coined by Jung in articulating his theory.

Jung's type theory emerged out of a period of professional and personal conflict in his own life. The editors of *The Collected Works of C. G. Jung* referred to these years (1913–1919) as Jung's "fallow period," in which no "real" work was completed due to his complete self-absorption. This prolonged crisis occurred partly as a result of his painful separation from Freud in 1913. Despite Jung's extreme disappointment over the loss of his mentor, he came to realize that the inability of two intelligent and sincere minds to agree on matters of importance was in itself of psychological interest. Jung also observed that a conflict had caused Freud to sever his relationship with another early and talented student, Alfred Adler. Thus, it was out of this professional and personal strife that Jung's work on typology was formulated.

Jung set out to examine the conflict between Freud, Adler, and himself on a typological basis. He concluded that the differences between them, which led to the breakdown in their relationships, were based on typological opposites at work. For example, he viewed the conflict between Freud and Adler as arising out of the problem of the opposite attitudes of extraversion and introversion. Thus, type theory emerged out of Jung's own struggles with personal relationships and his need to understand why those relationships broke down. The "fallow period" eventually bore fruit with the publication of *Psychological Types* in 1921, which set out his theory.

The Components of Typology

According to Jung, all people experience innate, biological dichotomies. He suggests that each person is born with three polarities, which are: extraversion and introversion, sensation and intuition, and thinking and feeling.

The first dichotomy represents one's attitude or orientation toward the world. Extraverted types are stimulated by the environment; their focus is on objects and people. Introverted types are stimulated by inner experiences; their focus is on concepts and ideas. Extraverts aim to be active, sociable, and expressive while introverts aim to be reflective, reserved, and quiet.

The second and third dichotomies, which Jung labels the "functions of consciousness," are sensation and intuition, thinking and feeling. The first two, sensation and intuition, he calls the "irrational functions," responsible for the "what" of our experience. (By "irrational" Jung means non-rational rather than contra-rational.) They are our functions of awareness. Sensation is concerned with facts, details, and the present; intuition with innovations, patterns, and the future. Sensing types are often practical, matter-of-fact, and realistic. Intuitive types are often imaginative, abstract, and theoretical. Sensation and intuition are polar opposites and cannot be used in the same instant.

Jung calls thinking and feeling the "rational functions" responsible for ordering our experience. One is concerned with the head, the other with the heart. The functions of thinking and feeling are not merely differences they are opposites and cannot be used at the same moment. When one uses the head, the heart is pushed aside, and vice versa. Thinking provides rational order through impersonal reasoning. Thinking types are often logical, analytical, and objective. Feeling provides rational order through personal impression. Feeling types are often empathic, compassionate, and subjective. Thus, each individual possesses the four functions of sensation, intuition, thinking, and feeling but exercises them in differing capacity and priority.

The functions of consciousness are given distinctive expression depending on whether one is introverted or extraverted. Jung's theory emphasizes the importance of the introversion-extraversion polarity. So, in *Psychological Types* he identifies eight types: introverted thinking, extraverted thinking, introverted feeling, extraverted feeling, introverted sensation, extraverted sensation, introverted intuition, and extraverted intuition.

Contributions of Myers and Briggs and Development of the MBTI

The Myers-Briggs Type Indicator (MBTI) was developed to test the psychological type theory of C. G. Jung and to put it to practical use. The instrument's designers were Katharine Cook Briggs and Isabel Briggs Myers who during the 1920s and 1930s made their own observations of human behavior that they believed corresponded with Jung's theories on typology. When World War II broke out, they envisioned their instrument as a tool that people could use in the future to prevent such disastrous conflicts. On a more personal level, Myers, whose husband was nearly her typological opposite, used typology to understand issues in her own marriage. Thus, the MBTI was constructed to build bridges between people.

In developing the instrument, Myers and Briggs expanded on Jung's three dichotomies: they took a part of Jung's theory that was implicit and made it explicit. For Jung, a person's psychological type contains one attitude toward the world (either extraversion or introversion) and a dominant function (either thinking, feeling, sensation, or intuition). In addition, a person has an auxiliary function that supports the dominant function. If the dominant function is a "rational function" (thinking or feeling), then the auxiliary function is an "irrational function" (sensation or intuition), and vice versa. The auxiliary function serves to give balance to the person. For example, a person might have extraverted sensation with thinking as the auxiliary function.

One of the problems of typological assessment is determining which of the functions is dominant and which is auxiliary. While it might be obvious that the person prefers sensation over intuition as the "irrational function" and that the person prefers thinking over feeling as the "rational function," it might not be clear whether the person prefers the "rational function" (thinking) or the "irrational function" (sensation) as the dominant function. This is where the MBTI makes a contribution by extending Jung's theory.

Myers and Briggs added an implied fourth dichotomy from Jung's writings, called the Judging-Perceiving (J–P) polarity. This dichotomy is concerned with the attitude taken toward the outer world. Judging types prefer to use Thinking or Feeling as the way of managing their extraverted (external) life. Perceiving types use Sensing or Intuition as the way of engaging their extraverted (external) life. Judging types typically have an organized life-style and are decisive. Perceiving types typically have a flexible life-style and are spontaneous. Once the J–P polarity is added, the dichotomies appear as follows:

Extraversion (E)	and	Introversion (I)
Sensing (S)[1]	and	Intuition (N)
Thinking (T)	and	Feeling (F)
Judging (J)	and	Perceiving (P)

Thus, the MBTI adds a final letter so that an EST is either an ESTJ or an ESTP. This innovation allows one to identify the dominant function. For extraverted types, like ESTs, the final letter added (J or P) indicates how one relates to the outer world. Since the outer world is where extraverts focus their attention and receive energy, the J or P indicates the dominant. Thus, for an ESTJ the dominant is the Judging function, Thinking; for an ESTP the dominant is the Perceiving function, Sensing.

But what about introverted types? For them, the reverse is true. For introverts, the dominant function is reserved for the internal world. The inner world is where introverts focus their attention and receive energy. Let's use the fourth letter to determine the dominant function of an IST. If the person is an

ISTJ, then the person uses the Judging (J) function, in this case Thinking, to relate to the outer world. Since it is the inner world, however, where the introvert focuses, Thinking is auxiliary rather than dominant. The other function recorded by the MBTI for the ISTJ is Sensing, which is the dominant function in this case.

Consider an ISTP. An ISTP relates to the outer world through the perceiving function, Sensing. Since an introvert, however, focuses attention and energy predominantly in the inner world, the judging function, in this case Thinking, is the dominant function. The key for using the Judging–Perceiving dichotomy is to understand that for introverts this dichotomy refers to the auxiliary function, and for extraverts this dichotomy refers to the dominant function.

Altogether there are sixteen psychological types in the MBTI inventory. This represents an expansion on Jung's theory that explicitly identified eight types. Today, the MBTI is the most widely used psychological instrument for identifying differences among normal people. Its purpose, of course, is to assist individuals in understanding themselves. Such knowledge is useful for understanding how one perceives and evaluates the world. The MBTI is used in many fields today: educators use the MBTI to improve teaching and learning; counselors use it to help clients with marriage difficulties or career selection; executives use it to help them understand managerial strengths and weaknesses; ministers use it to aid their understanding of the spiritual needs of different types. These types are represented by the sixteen combinations of the letters below:

ISTJ	ISFJ	INFJ	INTJ
ISTP	ISFP	INFP	INTP
ESTP	ESFP	ENFP	ENTP
ESTJ	ESFJ	ENFJ	ENTJ

Using Type in Moral Decision Making

This book extends the usage of the MBTI and type theory into the field of ethics. This is appropriate especially in light of the history of the development of typology. Jung, along with Myers and Briggs, believed that heightened awareness of oneself and of others would lead to more harmonious personal relationships and a more just society.

The book focuses on the four functions: Sensing, Intuition, Thinking, and Feeling. As noted, these functions are polarities of perception (S–N) and judgment (T–F). In type theory, people cannot stand outside of the framework of their own type. If differing types have innate ways of perceiving and evaluating the world, then this will extend to the realm of ethics. In making moral decisions, what we perceive and how we judge are crucial. Sensing types are likely to perceive moral dilemmas in ways dissimilar to Intuitive types. Sensing and Intuition are concerned with the *what* of our moral existence. They help us answer the question: *What should I do?* Thinking types are likely to arrive at ethical decisions in distinctively different ways than Feeling types. Thinking and Feeling are concerned with the *how* of moral evaluation. They help us answer the question: *How should I decide?* As polarities, these functions provide opposing ways of doing ethics. If we are to make moral perceptions and evaluations that are truly our own, they should arise from and find consistency with our underlying priorities and values as represented in our psychological type.

Pathways to Integrity divides ethical responses into four fundamental categories based on types differing. The function polarities, considered in their four possible combinations (ST, SF, NT, and NF), produce distinctive ways of arriving at moral decisions. We will explore ST Duty, SF Care, NT Justice, and NF Compassion.

This book will assist individuals in their ability to make conscious ethical decisions that reflect the integrity of their psychological type. It does this by:

1) introducing the reader to the moral dimensions of the psychological functions (chapters 2 and 3);

2) introducing the reader to major ethical theories as they relate to psychological type (chapter 4); and

3) providing a practical, dialectical method of moral decision making for specific psychological types (chapters 5 and 6).

Moral decision making which arises from our natural processes is likely to be good and useful to ourselves and to society. Decision making which is artificial and contrived is likely to be psychologically infectious to ourselves and to others. *Pathways to Integrity* aims to give confidence to those who lack awareness of their moral strengths and modesty to those who have blind spots in their moral reasoning. In gaining this awareness we will be better equipped to judge for ourselves what is right.

Chapter
Two

One day we will learn that the heart can never
be totally right if the head is totally wrong.
Only through the bringing together of head
and heart—intelligence and goodness—shall
man rise to a fulfillment of his true nature . . . .

— MARTIN LUTHER KING, JR.

The Moral Dimensions of the Thinking and Feeling Functions

The Functions of Option

C. G. Jung in his book *Psychological Types* calls *thinking* and *feeling* the "rational functions." The Myers-Briggs Type Indicator calls them the "judging functions." Jungian analyst John Beebe suggests that we adopt I. N. Marshall's phrase "functions of option" for them (Marshall 1968). The thinking and feeling functions of the psyche, then, are concerned with ordering our experience. They are our discriminating and evaluative functions. One uses the head, the other, the heart.

Isabel Briggs Myers and Mary H. McCaulley describe Thinking as:

> . . . the function that comes to a decision by linking ideas together through logical connections. Thinking relies on principles of cause and effect and tends to be objective and impersonal in the application of reason to a decision. Persons who are primarily oriented toward Thinking are likely to develop characteristics associated with this way of arriving at conclusions: analytical inclination, objectivity, concern with principles of justice and fairness, criticality, an impassive and dispassionate demeanor, and an orientation to time that is linear, that is, concerned with connections from the past through the present and toward the future. (Myers, McCaulley, Quenk, Hammer 1998, p. 24)

Myers and McCaulley describe Feeling as:

> . . . the function by which one comes to decisions by weighing relative values and merits of the issues. Feeling relies on an understanding of personal values and group values; thus it is more subjective than thinking. Because

values are subjective and personal, persons making judgments with the feeling function are more likely to be
attuned to the values of others as well as to their own values and feelings. They try to understand people and to
anticipate and take into account the effects of the decision
at hand and on the people involved and on what is important to them. They have a concern with the human as
opposed to the technical aspects of problems, a desire for
affiliation, warmth, and harmony, a time orientation that
includes preservation of enduring values. (Myers et al
1998, pp. 24–25)

Our Thinking and Feeling functions are extremely important
in our moral deliberations regarding: *How should I decide between
right and wrong?*

A Dialectic Between Thinking and Feeling

According to Beebe (1995), "The Western conception of [ethics]
emerges out of a philosophical dialectic between thinking and
feeling functions . . ." (p. 32). While it is popular to interpret
Jung's theories of functions in terms of "gifts differing," (that is
the idea that we all have different gifts to be exercised accord-
ingly—some as Thinking types, some as Feeling types, etc.), this
reading may miss something important regarding moral decision
making.

In *Jung's Typology in Perspective,* Angelo Spoto points out
that "in order to follow the thread of Jung's typological work
throughout Jung's career, it is helpful and important now to
draw a distinction between the *problem of differences* and the
problem of opposites in Jung's book *Psychological Types*" (pp. 6–7,
italics added). While the popularization of the MBTI has led to
the common usage of the term *differences* to define the various
psychological functions, some of the energy and fervor that is
germane to Jung's original work is missed if one only considers
the problem of differences. Differences connote that things are
distinct or separate without noting how different or how separate
they are from each other. One could use differences to talk about
hair color—this one is blond and that one is brown. Or language

—this one speaks Spanish and that one speaks English. Hair colors blonde and brown, as languages Spanish and English, are not opposites. They are simply different. *The American-Heritage Dictionary of the English Language* defines *opposites,* however, as "facing the other way; moving or tending away from each other; *altogether* different, as in nature, quality, or significance" (s.v. "opposite," italics added). What should be kept in mind here is that the functions of Thinking and Feeling are not merely differences, they are opposites. They are as opposite as night and day, black and white. Furthermore, Jung argues that one cannot use both of these functions at the same time. When one uses his head, his heart is pushed aside, and vice versa. They can be engaged alternatively, but not at the same moment.

Beebe states that ethical theory in Western culture emerges out of a dialectic between the judging functions of Thinking and Feeling. A *dialectic* is "a method of argument or exposition that systematically weighs contradictory facts or ideas with the view to the resolution of their real or apparent contradictions" (*Ibid.*, s.v. "dialectic"). This process is associated with the German philosopher Hegel who proposed that truth is reached by a continuing dialectic. How does one engage in moral decision making as a dialectic between the opposite functions of Thinking and Feeling?

An Ethic of Justice or an Ethic of Care?

In recent years, this dialectic in the United States has been between an *ethic of justice* based on Thinking and an *ethic of care* based on Feeling. In the 1970s, American educator and psychologist Lawrence Kohlberg published his findings that maintained that moral development was largely dependent on logical reasoning ability. Through interviews with individuals at various stages of maturity, he proposed that everyone has potential for development from lower stages to higher stages of morality. These stages are sequential and each new stage represents a higher system of logic for deciding what is the just way to solve a moral problem. Kohlberg believed that *justice* was the goal of all moral decision making. Kohlberg's work and that of the *cognitive-development psychologists* that followed have had a major impact on ethics education in America.

Unlike Kohlberg, care ethicists regard Feeling, rather than Thinking or formal logic, as the bottom-line. Modern care ethics, though rooted in David Hume's virtue ethics, was developed primarily from the work of Carol Gilligan's study of women's moral development. Gilligan, professor of education at Harvard University, found that women tend to be more context-oriented than men. She argued that Kohlberg's model, which placed a high value on abstract principles and reasoning ability for moral evaluations, was deficient since women tended to make moral evaluations based on feelings and relationships. Men, she said, tended to be principle-oriented while women tended to be more personal-oriented. Gilligan coined the term "care perspective," which contrasted with Kohlberg's ethic of justice.

Many care ethicists believe that the ethic of care is "essentially feminine." (Noddings 1984) This is also a widely held notion as is reflected in the 1992 bestseller *Men are from Mars; Women are from Venus* by John Gray. Gray writes: "A woman's sense of self is defined through her feelings and the quality of her relationships" (p. 18). Men, on the other hand, "are more interested in 'objects' and 'things' rather than people and feelings" (p. 16).

Yet there is evidence that the preference for Feeling over Thinking (or vice versa), as a way of ethical decision making, cuts across gender lines. Statistics suggest "females have relatively more F types and males have more T types" (Myers and McCaulley, 1985, p. 45). In fact, Isabel Myers' 1962 estimate that about 60 percent of males in the United States prefer the Thinking function and that about 65 percent of females in the United States prefer the Feeling function (*Ibid.*), has largely held constant. The National Representative Sample data in the 1998 MBTI Manual, show 56.5 percent of males prefer Thinking and 75.5 percent of females prefer Feeling (Myers et al, 1998, p. 298). What these statistics suggest, then, is that a significant though smaller portion of men prefer the Feeling function and a significant though smaller portion of women prefer the Thinking function. Some men are Feeling types, just as some women are Thinking types.

Beebe points out that the justice-care debate ultimately derives from Jung. Jung gives the perspectives that Gilligan labels "care" and "justice" the names *eros* and *logos*. Eros is "the need to cultivate caring for the wholeness of others as well as of oneself" (Beebe 1995, p. 81). Logos, in contradistinction, "means the capacity to differentiate and discriminate, implying a conception of justice by which such discriminations can be made" (*Ibid.*).

Spock versus McCoy

Two of the main characters in the television series *Star Trek* embody the contention between head and heart. First officer Mr. Spock, a Vulcan with pointed ears, makes all decisions on the basis of logic. The Vulcan civilization made a religion of logic. In doing so, it was necessary to eliminate all emotions. Spock is emotionless. He doesn't smile, laugh, cry, or get angry. Emotions are considered a hindrance to true understanding; they get in the way. Spock is often heard to say, "But Captain, that is illogical." In Spock's view, if it is not logical, it is wrong. Spock, as a caricature of the Thinking type, arrives at equitable decisions by applying an absolute standard of cold, impersonal logic.

Throughout the series Spock and McCoy, the ship's physician, are often at odds. Dr. McCoy is Spock's nemesis and chief critic. He pokes fun at him, belittles him, and threatens him. McCoy does not trust Spock's use of logic in solving problems and is usually annoyed when Spock calculates the odds. McCoy is the good, old-fashioned doctor who responds to people's needs when they cannot take care of themselves. He is a folksy humanitarian who, though gruff, has a big heart. His domain is care. McCoy is a caricature of the Feeling type who weighs matters of importance with a warm concern for the welfare of others.

As Spock and McCoy are the principal advisors to Kirk, the ship's captain, so Thinking and Feeling are the principal advisors to Westerners as they make ethical decisions. A dialectical approach will value these opposites in their advisory roles.

Landry versus Lombardi

In the early 1960s, professional football, through the medium of television, was on the verge of replacing baseball as the most popular American sport. The established Green Bay Packers hired a fiery young coach named Vince Lombardi while the upstart Dallas Cowboys hired a brainy young coach named Tom Landry. Both men, who had served as assistant coaches together for the NFL Champion New York Giants, became legends. Lombardi would win six NFL championships at Green Bay (including the first two Super Bowls). The NFL now awards its annual Super Bowl champion the "The Lombardi Trophy." Landry, on the other hand, forged the Dallas Cowboys into one of the premier sports franchises in the world. The Cowboys became "America's Team" under Landry as they played in five Super Bowls and set an NFL record of twenty consecutive winning seasons. Landry coached the Cowboys for an amazing twenty-nine years.

Lombardi and Landry were polar opposites. One fire, the other ice. Lombardi, the Feeling type, coached through the tactics of hate and love, fear and loyalty. He created a family in his ball club, with him as the patriarch. His orders were unquestioned. His players believed in him; they loved him. He roamed the sideline during a game, constantly encouraging or berating, his expressions of anger or joy, depression or elation visible on his face.

Landry, on the other hand, was the calculating and cool Thinking type. He was called "a football genius," the inventor of the 4–3 defense and the multiple-set offense. Landry was always changing the game, and was ahead of his time. His players believed in his system; they had faith in their coach as a strategist, not as a cheerleader. During a game, Landry rarely displayed any emotion. One of the first to wear a headset to communicate with his coaches in the press box, the only time he spoke was when he called the play. (Landry called all of the plays before it was the norm.) He rarely got close to his players, who described him as aloof and stoic, yet respected him.

Synthesis of Heart and Head

Is it possible that one person can include both a Spock and McCoy within himself? Can one be both Lombardi-like and Landry-like? Jung argues that one cannot use the functions of Feeling and Thinking at the same time. However, he does insist that in order to be whole (or "individuated") it is necessary to exercise all of the functions. He writes, "Although every act of conscious realization is at least a step forward on the road to individuation, to the 'making whole' of the individual, the integration of the personality is unthinkable without the responsible, and that means *moral*, relation of the parts to one another, just as the constitution of a state is impossible without mutual relations between its members" (p. 13, italics added). Ethical wholeness results in part from the dialectical conversation between head and heart.

Both Kohlberg and Gilligan eventually conclude that the ethics of justice and the ethics of care are not mutually exclusive but rather complimentary. Each perspective has strengths and weaknesses. The justice perspective centers on the ideal of equity for the larger community. This detachment can sometimes lead, however, to a lack of awareness of local human need. The care perspective focuses on our relationships to each other and to the particular needs of individuals. This contextualization can sometimes miss, however, the broader issues of justice and equality.

How, then, should we decide matters of right and wrong? A dialectical approach that weighs matters with both the heart and the head is likely to produce a synthesis conducive to the best ethical decision. This dialectic, prevalent in Western culture, and dominating cognitive structural theories during the last several decades, is familiar to most Americans.

Chapter Three

Let a man not do what his own sense of righteousness tells him not to do, and let him not desire what his sense of righteousness tells him not to desire;—to act thus is all he has to do.

— MENCIUS

The Moral Dimensions of the Sensing and Intuition Functions

The Functions of the Given

C. G. Jung calls *sensation* and *intuition* the "irrational" or non-rational functions. The Myers-Briggs Type Indicator uses the term "perceiving functions," and John Beebe suggests we adopt Marshall's phrase "functions of the given" (Marshall 1968, pp. 1–32). The Sensing and Intuitive functions of the psyche, then, are concerned with the "what" of our experience. They are our functions of awareness: Sensing is concerned with the present facts, Intuition with future possibilities.

Isabel Briggs Myers and Mary H. McCaulley describe the Sensing function as:

> . . . observable by way of the senses. Sensing establishes what exists. Because the senses can bring to awareness only what is occurring in the present moment, persons oriented toward sensing perception tend to focus on the immediate experience available to their fives senses. They, therefore, often develop characteristics associated with this awareness such as enjoying the present moment, realism, acute powers of observation, memory for details, and practicality. (Myers et al 1998, p. 24)

Myers and McCaulley describe the Intuitive function as the:

> . . . perception of possibilities, meanings, and relationships by way of insight. Jung characterized intuition as perception by way of the unconscious. Intuitions may come to the surface of consciousness suddenly, as a "hunch," the sudden perception of a pattern in seemingly unrelated events.

Intuition permits perception beyond what is visible to the senses, including possible future events. People who prefer Intuition may develop the characteristics that can follow from emphasis on intuition and become imaginative, theoretical, abstract, future oriented, or creative. Persons oriented toward Intuition may also become so intent on pursuing possibilities that they may overlook actualities. . . . When the sensing function is used to perceive an apple, a person might describe it as "juicy," "crisp," "red," or "white with black seeds." When the Intuitive function is used to perceive the same apple, a person may say "William Tell," "How to keep the doctor away," "Roast pig," or "My grandmother's famous pie." (Myers et al 1998, p. 24)

Through Sensing and Intuition, "we can get a *factual readout* on the status of our integrity and a *vision of its potential* for development." (Beebe 1995, p. 24, italics added) These psychological functions help us answer the important ethical question of: *What should I do?*

A Dialectic between Sensing and Intuition

While Beebe suggests that the Western conception of ethics emerges out of the Thinking–Feeling dialectic, he says "the Eastern conception of [ethics] is a traditional spiritual attitude based on a dialectic between the sensation and intuitive functions in the practical interpretation of experience" (p. 32). Most Americans are familiar with the head-heart struggle of daily life. This struggle occurs on a level playing field since statistics indicate that Americans are nearly evenly divided between those who prefer Thinking and those who prefer Feeling as evaluative functions. Not so with Sensing and Intuition. The data from the MBTI suggest that approximately 73.3 percent of Americans prefer Sensing over Intuition (Myers et al 1998, p. 298). So this playing field will not be level in American culture as these opposites compete.

It is again helpful to remember that the function pairs are polar opposites and not merely differences. Jung argues that the interplay of the opposites is essential for psychic health and well-being. Where one function dominates, an imbalance occurs. This imbalance can occur in a culture as well as in an individual. If nearly three-fourths of Americans prefer Sensing over Intuition, what imbalance would one expect from a cultural perspective? Another way to ask the question is: What are the biases of the culture?

Notice the following characteristics that develop from the Sensing and Intuitive functions. In doing so, consider which function is most valued in the fields of business, education, and politics in Western culture.

Sensing (S)	Intuition (N)
proof	possibilities
facts	vision
law	fate
cause	chance
result	potential
certainty	wonder
know	guess
concentrate	dream
evident	latent
sensible	mindful

In a bottom-line, results-oriented, technologically-based society, the preference of institutions for the abilities of Sensing types is apparent.

In the East, however, the conception of ethics issues from a dialectic between Sensing and Intuition. This dialectic is no more clearly seen than in the compensatory traditional religions of China—Confucianism and Taoism. These two religions provide a

Figure 1

unity of opposites for their adherents who sometimes belong to both traditions at the same time. Many Chinese attempt to harmonize the opposite characteristics of Confucianism and Taoism in their individual lives. This union of opposites is best illustrated in the ancient Chinese symbol known as the *Tai chi* (figure 1) in which the two cosmic forces the *yin* and *yang* interact.

Confucianism, which rules in the public sphere, is especially concerned with *li*, manners, and *yi*, right behavior. It is the way of routine, ceremonial rites, propriety, and step-by-step procedures. To be morally good, one must cultivate and honor the values of the culture. Out of respect for parents, elders, and government, one develops into a *chun-zu*, or gentleman. Confucius says: "There are four components in a proper man's doing: He is reverent in his personal conduct, scrupulously honorable in serving his prince, considerate in provisioning the people, and just in employing them" (Analects 13:3). Thus, one's moral obligations emerge out of the particular roles that one is assigned. Each role requires certain social duties: rulers should behave as rulers, parents as parents, children as children.[1] Confucianism exhibits a strong Sensing, here-and-now orientation, with little or no intuitive projection into future alternatives or possibilities.

Taoism, on the other hand, rules in the private sphere. The moral stance of Taoism is perhaps best expressed in the concept of *wu wei*. *Wu wei*, or "doing without doing" means taking no action contrary to nature. In sports it is the equivalent of being "in the zone" or "playing unconscious." It is the carefree, natural, simple way of life. Taoists attempt to align themselves with the unnameable original force called the *Tao*. The Taoist sage Lao Tzu says:

> Humans model themselves on earth,
> Earth on heaven,
> Heaven on the way,
> And the way on that which is naturally so.
>
> (*Tao-te Ching*, verse 25)

This natural way contrasts with the cultured way of Confucianism. The Taoist does not cultivate his nature in order to become the educated gentleman. He lives and lets live. This strong Intuitive, long-term view of life, with little or no immediate concern for the practical business (or busy-ness) at hand, is expressed in the Taoist image of flowing water. It goes around all obstacles and gently erodes all obstacles rather than deliberately attacking them. In the end, all is accomplished.

Taoism as the Intuitive ethical path and Confucianism as the Sensing ethical path are illustrative of the Eastern dialectic to which Beebe points.

Solar Conscience /Lunar Conscience

In *Solar Conscience/Lunar Conscience: An Essay on the Psychological Foundations of Morality, Lawfulness, and the Sense of Justice,* Jungian analyst Murray Stein examines the bipolar nature of morality. His book provides the Western reader with insight into the moral dialectic prevalent in Eastern culture. Instead of the more familiar head versus heart dialectic involving the functions of option, Stein provides a less familiar solar versus lunar dialectic involving the functions of the given, Sensing and Intuition.

The primary intent of *Solar Conscience/Lunar Conscience* is to examine the role of conscience in ethical decision making. Stein describes conscience as "a gut reaction . . . not the product of rational thought and reflection" (p. 1). Here the suggestion is that the dialectic occurs between the functions of perception rather than the functions of judgment. This is tricky since conscience does, in fact, render a judgment. Conscience, according to Stein, "seems always to confront a person with negative restrictions and positive demands . . ." (p. 2). Yet our conscience is not something that we as individuals create or control. Our conscience does not arise from the deliberations of our logical reasoning or from the affect of our personal feelings. Rather, it is a given. It is as Stein says, "a gut reaction." It is a voice within us which arises spontaneously. When the voice is heard it creates ambivalence for us since it may suggest we take a course of action different from what we want. "I want this, but it demands that" (p. 2). Stein describes these two consciences in the following ways.

Solar conscience speaks in and through and for what Jung called the persona. Through this structure, a person incorporates and embodies the values and expectations of parents, teachers, religious figures, and peers. Solar conscience is therefore constituted by culture, and it takes its place within the psychic matrix as the reinforcing backbone of dominant cultural patterns.

When one examines the content of solar conscience, one finds that the values it contains have been carefully laid down and refined through a long collective tradition. Such values can usually be found written down and codified in scriptures and in books of conduct if the culture is literate and in stories and myths if it is oral. Solar conscience can be imaged . . . as a masculine authority figure or a policeman, whose job is to maintain structures, to preserve the peace, and to thwart aggression, sexuality, and other impulse . . . . (p. 17, italics added)

Individuals who prefer Sensing over Intuition, the majority of Americans, will be more likely to hear the voice of solar conscience. It will be heard clearly.

Lunar conscience, on the other hand, will be conceived as the oracular voice of nature . . . . Here conscience speaks for an intuition of cosmic order that permeates the natural world and includes humans as conscious creatures within that world. It speaks out of and for . . . instinct, body, *materia*. Lunar conscience addresses us not in the patriarchal traditions or through our culturally established moral systems but through the unconscious, in dreams, in complexes, in spontaneous happenings, through instinctual hungers, and also through the inhibitions that lie buried within those hungers. (p. 19, italics added)

Individuals who prefer Intuition over Sensing will be more likely to hear the voice of lunar conscience which speaks through the unconscious. This voice in Western culture will not be the favored voice. As indicated earlier, this dialectic is not being contested on a level playing field in America. To summarize, solar conscience is responsible to society; lunar conscience is responsible to nature. Each give us the "what" of our ethical inquiry; they tell us what we seek or what we should do.

Scotty and Captain Kirk

Scotty, the ship's engineer of *Star Trek,* is a devotee of the practical and verifiable, a Sensing type. He is the down-to-earth, hands-on mechanic whose sole interest is the engine of the *Enterprise.* Scotty has little taste for idle talk, abstract ideas, or philosophizing. He does, however, know the details of the ship forward and backward. On many occasions, the ship is saved from destruction though his meticulous engineering skills.

Though Captain Kirk is much more complex and well-rounded than the other characters on the *Enterprise,* his use of Intuition is legendary. Karin Blair discusses Kirk's use of Intuition in her book *Meaning in Star Trek.* She analyzes a scene in which the ship's landing party on an unknown planet is confronted by a vapor which has a sweet honey-like aroma. Kirk, like the rest of the party, smells the sweet aroma but uses his Intuition to measure his response. When they first detect the smell, Spock suggests that it must be spring-time on the planet. Kirk, however, responds with associations from his memory, recalling that he had faced a similar situation eleven years earlier. The mysterious vapor eventually attacks the crew and then takes off through the galaxy, leaving no scent or trail. While the crew wonders where it has gone, Kirk intuitively knows. He decides on a hunch to travel across the galaxy to find it. Relying only on Intuition, he locates the vapor and destroys it.

Blair points out that while most of the *Star Trek* characters have a dominant way of interacting with the world, Kirk

> . . . as a whole person has access within himself to emotion and intuition, intellect and sensation. He can encounter the world either through sensation by registering data which can convey concrete reality or through intuition by grasping the possibilities hidden in the background of the concrete. He can process or digest the fruit of this encounter by means of the intellect or rational analysis, or through emotional evaluation, which tells him how or to what extent something is important. (pp. 63–64)

Jung argues that such wholeness, while rare, is the task of all human beings. In moral decision making, the use of all four psychological functions enables us to be the reliable captain of our own ship as we encounter new frontiers.

Phil Jackson's *Sacred Hoops*

Phil Jackson, coach of the Chicago Bulls and the Los Angeles Lakers of the NBA, won six NBA championships with the Bulls and set the standard for excellence in the sport. He went on to become a winner with the Lakers as well. In his book *Sacred Hoops* (1995), Coach Jackson reveals a coaching style that is highly intuitive. While professional coaching has become a scientifically-based numbers game of interchangeable parts in which the head coach is a "control-oholic" business executive, Jackson's style is that of an artist and shaman. Though all good coaches use the function of Intuition, Jackson is the example of this function *par excellence*. He is a maverick in a profession dominated by the style of Sensing types.

Jackson contrasts his intuitive style of coaching with his Sensing-oriented assistant Charley Rosen. He writes:

> Rosen and I were a good match. He saw everything in black and white; I saw infinite gradations of gray. He was obsessed with pinpointing the exact moment when everything turned to dung and who was to blame—more often than not, a referee. I was more interested in the quality of the team's energy as it ebbed and flowed, and figuring out what lessons could be learned when disaster struck. As my wife likes to say, I can "smell a rose in a pile of manure." (p. 62)

Jackson sees his role as cultivating an atmosphere in which the creative intuition of each player and of the team itself is unleashed during a basketball game. In this atmosphere a trust develops at "a deep level" whereby players know "instinctively how their teammates" will respond in pressure situations (p. 18). For Jackson, being aware of the whole (N) is more important than being fundamentally sound in specific skills of the game (S). Through intuition, Jackson taps the individual unconscious of each player and the collective unconscious of the team.

While Coach Jackson's methods are unorthodox, they are highly effective. Note the ways that he creates an environment out of which court awareness can emerge. (1) Sacred Space. The locker room is an "inner sanctum . . . a sacred space adorned with Native American totems and other symbolic objects . . ." (p. 11). Such spaces are necessary for creating a state by which intuitive processes can work. (2) Meditation. As an adherent of the Zen practice of sitting meditation, *zazen,* Jackson testifies that "I was far more effective when my mind was clear and I wasn't playing with an agenda of some kind, like scoring a certain number of points or showing up one of my opponents" (p. 50). He believes that the "quieting of the mind," so that one does not "think too much," pays important dividends on the basketball court (p. 35). This mind-state is important in order for players to achieve "an awareness of the whole" (p. 35). (3) Visualization. Jackson teaches his players to "code the image of a successful move into [their] visual memory so that when a similar situation emerged in a game" they can perform it unconsciously (p. 38). Intuition, unlike the other functions, arises out of our unconscious. Through visualization, his players tap the enormous powers of their unconscious. (4) Group Intelligence. Jackson, in alchemical fashion, sees his task as transforming the team into something greater than its parts. He believes that if "every single member of the group" accepts the same vision of reality (which means accepting their specific roles on the court) then the "group intelligence" will be greater than that of the coach or even that of a Michael Jordan (p. 100). Again, this intelligence does not arise out of any one person's conscious but arises from the group's unconscious.

Jackson's *Sacred Hoops* is an excellent experiential account of the relationship between spirituality and sport and offers insight in how to coach and manage by way of Intuition. It should be noted, however, before we get carried away with his intuitive genius, that Jackson seeks to balance his approach by hiring assistants (like Charley Rosen or Tex Winters), Sensing types who master and teach the nuts and bolts of component skills. Assistant Tex Winters, in fact, is credited with inventing the Chicago Bulls famed "triangle offense." Head coaches who are Sensing types abound in the ranks of professional basketball. Technical greats like Jerry Sloan and Pat Riley demonstrate Sensing aptitude measured in consistent NBA success.

Synthesis of Sensing and Intuition

Again, it is Beebe's contention that the Western conception of ethics involves a dialectic between the Thinking and Feeling functions while the Eastern conception of ethics involves a dialectic between the Sensing and Intuitive functions. This "Eastern" dialectic applied to moral behavior is less familiar to Westerners who have a cultural imbalance related to Sensing and Intuition. As functions of the given, Sensing and Intuition may be thought of as *differing consciences,* "gut reactions," either responsible to society or responsible to Nature. Stein calls them our "solar" and "lunar" consciences. In chapter 4, I will use the terms *conscience of principle* and *conscience of potential* to describe these particular and differing perspectives. These consciences based on Sensing and Intuition help us to answer the important ethical question of: What should I do? Since most Americans prefer Sensing over Intuition, it seems likely that a conscience arising out of social rules, a conscience of principle, will be more prevalent in the United States.

The United State's position as the world's sole superpower reminds us that a culture's focus on Sensing pays huge dividends in technological and material success. Sensing rules! Yet intuitive geniuses can be found in all professions in American life today. Phil Jackson's unorthodox yet successful style is a reminder that the unconscious is a powerful and creative phenomenon of our lives. Jung, an NT, had a preference for the function of Intuition over all others.

In conclusion, we are reminded that, as captains of our own ethical ship, it is useful to receive advice from all hands on board. Like Kirk, at the center of the *Enterprise,* we have the capacity to listen to Sensing and Intuition, as well as Thinking and Feeling, in making crucial decisions that shape our world.

Chapter Four

**THOUGHT WITHOUT PRACTICE IS EMPTY,
PRACTICE WITHOUT THOUGHT IS BLIND.**

— KWAME NKRUMAH

Consciences Differing:
Doing What's Right or
Seeking the Good

Introduction

In the previous chapters, it was suggested that the functions of the given (S–N) assist us in answering the question: What should I do? And the functions of option (T–F) assist us in answering the question: How should I decide? Most of the major ethical theories of Western civilization can be categorized according to how these two questions are answered.

"What should I do?" There are two principal ways to answer this question. The way we answer will depend on the kind of conscience we possess. If we have a *conscience of potential,* we will consider the future implications of our actions. "What will happen if I do a certain thing?" Here *we are seeking the good.* The conscience of potential demands that we "seek the good" for the future. Intuitive types are likely to answer the question of "What should I do?" in this way. If, on the other hand, we have a *conscience of principle,* we will consider the act alone. "Is the thing I do right or wrong, regardless of the consequences?" Here *we are doing what's right.* The conscience of principle demands that we "do what's right" in the present. Sensing types are likely to answer the question of "What should I do?" in this way.[1]

The second question we ask is "How should I decide?" This is a question of option. The polarity in this case will be between the head and the heart, between Thinking and Feeling. If an Intuitive type "seeks the good" for future results, does he do it with his head or his heart? If a Sensing type "does what's right" in the present situation, does she decide the course of action based on Thinking or Feeling?

This chapter connects C. G. Jung's typological theory to some of the major ethical theories of Western civilization. The presupposition is that the ethical theory which is a "fit" for the person will be based on his or her typology.

Part I
The Conscience of Principle (S): Doing What's Right

Sensing types, with their focus on the present, take an ethical stance of *"doing what's right,"* expressing a conscience of principle. Their conscience tells them what behavior is appropriate in the moment. The formal study of this phenomenon is known as deontology. Deontology is the study of moral obligation based on principle. Deontological theories are "duty-oriented;" their focus is on the act itself rather than the value it brings into existence. Deontologists argue that one has an obligation to act in a certain way because it is the right thing to do. Keeping promises, telling the truth, respecting others, honoring one's parents are viewed as right in themselves. These theories focus on the present, evaluating the correctness of the concrete action (S) rather than the hypothetical future consequences of the act (N). The conscience given to these types is a conscience of principle.

One of the most famous examples of a deontological approach to ethics in religious literature is found in the Hindu *Bhagavad Gita*. In this epic, the warrior *Arjuna* faces a moral dilemma. He is leading his troops to battle against an aggressing enemy when he is paralyzed by the thought that the consequences of his action may bring destruction to family and foe. He laments,

> . . . What is this crime I am planning . . . ? Murder most hateful, Murder of brothers! (*Bhagavad Gita* 1:44–47)

In his anxiety, he asks God for help. When God appears in the form of his chariot driver, He tells *Arjuna* that he must uphold his social obligations as a warrior:

What is this weakness? It is beneath you. Is it for nothing
men call you the foe-consumer? Shake off this cowardice,
Arjuna. Stand up. (*Bhagavad Gita* 2:35)

To not respond to the call of duty as a warrior would be
shameful. God continues by telling Arjuna that though he cannot
know the results of his action, he must act as duty bids:

Perform every action with your heart fixed on [God].
Renounce attachment to the fruits. Be even-tempered in
success and failure . . . . Work done with anxiety about
results is far inferior to work done without such anxiety, in
the calm of self-surrender. (*Bhagavad Gita* 2:47–53)

In other words, to do one's duty with a pure heart without
considering the results of one's action is the highest ethical
approach to life. The message of the *Bhagavad Gita* is clear:
despite the probable good or evil that one's action may bring, it
is morally prudent to execute one's duty. This is the conscience of
principle.

Sensing types are likely to find value in deontological
approaches since they are often culture bearers who focus primarily on day-to-day events. Like Arjuna, they are likely to hear and
act on the conscience of principle, the moral duty of culture and
law. Sensing combined with Thinking (ST) or with Feeling (SF) is
likely to produce distinctive ways of morally evaluating present
situations.

ST Duty

"Duty is the need to act out of respect for the law."
— IMMANUEL KANT

Summary: Doing the right thing consistently.
Best at: Minimizing or eliminating ambiguity and uncertainty; making objective rules.

Moral Considerations of the ST Type. STs are typically realists with a penchant for details and facts. They tend to value opinions that they view as unbiased, objective, detached, careful, analytical, and impersonal. Subjective Feeling is often eliminated. Their reasoning tends to be linear and causal with conclusions following directly from premises. In this way, clear-cut results are thought to be obtained provided one follows the correct sequential line of thinking. Such procedural rigor may at times seem legalistic to others. When STs believe they are right, they may be very direct, even brutally honest with their opinions. In making ethical decisions, they tend to value duty and fairness.

ST commitments usually lead them toward solid citizenship in communities. Their consistent and responsible devotion to leading productive lives is highly valued in their work places, religious organizations, associations, and families. Duty to various institutions is often their hallmark since they tend to be reliable and loyal. STs attend to the conscience of principle, hearing clearly their community's call to do the right thing.

STs usually believe that there is a right and a wrong in every situation. Once STs decide what is right, then their action often becomes a matter of living in accordance with that reality. The values of childhood or youth are often the values of adulthood for many STs. They may question moral precepts which they hold to be true but only when they directly contradict other precepts to which they adhere. Inconsistency of belief is morally intolerable for most STs. Because of this, others may see them as obstinate or parochial. STs tend to thrive in places where there are reliable and uniform rules which lead them to do the right thing day in and day out. In conclusion, ST morality is best at making objective rules or standards which minimize or eliminate ambiguity and uncertainty. This allows them to do the right thing consistently.

An ST Ethical Theory: Immanuel Kant's Unconditional Duty. German philosopher Immanuel Kant, one of the greatest thinkers in Western culture, made a lasting contribution in the area of ethics. Kant argues that ethics has nothing to do with satisfying a justifiable end. Results are irrelevant. In fact, if one considers the results of one's actions, this disqualifies the act as morally correct. The only motive for ethical conduct is a strict and pure sense of duty and not a desire for an intended outcome. The statement "You ought to treat your neighbor fairly, if you want him to treat you fairly" is not an example of a moral state-ment. Kant would say, "You ought to treat your neighbor fairly, period." Moral statements never have conditions attached. This he calls the principle of the "absolute imperative." This principle is founded on logical reasoning (T) alone.

The absolute imperative is an unconditional command which Kant states as follows: "Act only according to that *maxim* by which you can at the same time will that it should become a *universal law*" (p. 39, italics added). These maxims derive from the ST functions. (1) A maxim is a subjective rule according to which we determine behavior (S). "Don't cheat" is a maxim. (2) Each maxim is founded on logic (T), independent of any future outcome (N). In this way it will meet the test of universality. It would not be logical to state, "Don't cheat, unless cheating is the only way you can win the game." For Kant, cheating is always wrong.

Kant makes a number of important points to consider when making moral decisions. Ethicist Lawrence Hinman summarizes Kant's contributions as follows:

1) **The admirability of acting from duty (S).** Most of us

can agree that "there is something morally admirable about people who do the right thing, because it is their duty" (p. 212). Doing the right thing is often difficult and we can affirm those who have "the courage to go beyond narrow self-interest and do what is right for its own sake . . ." (p. 212).

2) **The evenhandedness of morality (T).** "This idea is stated most powerfully as a negative injunction to ourselves: we are not permitted to make an exception of the laws of morality just in order to benefit ourselves or those we care about" (p. 212). Such consistency becomes a check on our tendency to justify our actions when we permit exceptions.

3) **Respecting other persons.** "Without a doubt, one of Kant's key insights into the moral life was his insistence that we treat other people as ends-in-themselves, that we respect them as autonomous beings capable of reasoning and of making choices based on the results of that reasoning" (p. 212). This stance runs counter to intuitive tendencies in which the ends sometimes justify the means. Thus, the strength of Kantian ethics is found in duty-based Sensing and consistent, impartial Thinking.

Hinman also offers two important criticisms of Kant, noting where he misses the mark.

(1) The role of Feeling (F) in the moral life. Kant neglects moral integration by dismissing feelings from having any vital role in moral decision making. "Emotions, for Kant, are like forces that sweep over us, threatening to overwhelm our commitment to the good and to distort our vision of what is right" (p. 213).[2] Jung, however, believes that Feeling is as important as Thinking in our evaluation of the world around us. Such exclusion of a significant human function from decision making is psychologically dubious.

(2) The place of consequences (N). Here he goes too far in his refusal to consider the results of one's actions. How can one be morally responsible if consequences are totally ignored (pp. 213–214)?

How would Kant respond? A man with a family finds himself forced to borrow money in order to pay the bills. Instead of going to a bank that will surely refuse him the loan because of his bankruptcy, he goes to a neighbor. The neighbor says he will give him the money he needs but only if he agrees to pay him back within three months. The man knows that he will not be able to repay the neighbor in this amount of time. He also knows that he must pay the bills to support his family. Should he make a promise to the neighbor that he knows he cannot keep?

Kant writes:

> Now assuming he does decide to do so, the [logic] of his actions would be as follows: When I believe myself to be in need of money, I will borrow money and promise to repay it, although I know I shall never do so. Now this principle of self-love . . . may very well be compatible with his whole future welfare, but the question is whether it is right. He changes the pretension of self-love into a universal law and then puts the question: How would it be if my [logic] became a universal law? He immediately sees that it could never hold as a universal law of nature and be consistent with itself; rather it must necessarily contradict itself. For the universality of a law which says that anyone who believes himself to be in need could promise what he pleased with the intention of not fulfilling it would make the promise itself and the end to be accomplished by it impossible; no one would believe what was promised to him but would only laugh at any such assertion as vain pretense. (pp. 40–41)

ST RULE OF THUMB

ST morality, with its conscience of principle, answers the question "What should I do?" with "Do the right thing" no matter what the consequences to you or to others (S). ST morality answers "How should I decide?" with "Use your head" objectively and impersonally (T).

SF Care

A promise is a promise.

Summary: Doing the right thing by serving others.
Best at: Attending to the practical needs of individuals.

Moral Considerations of the SF Type. SFs are typically caring and sensitive people who express their devotion to others in immediate and concrete ways. Their tendency toward personal helpfulness is manifested in their morality, which is action-oriented. SFs often are first to volunteer to meet the practical and pressing needs of individuals with whom they have a relationship. By expressing their care in tangible and personal ways, their value commitments are easily observed. SFs tend to be extremely loyal to those they love and care for. This commitment to the well-being of others becomes the first and sometimes only consideration in their moral evaluations.

SFs are likely to fulfill the culture's expectations of them in terms of marriage, work, and other social expectations. They tend to like structured settings in which they know what is appropriate action for specific situations. In this way, SFs are often the culture bearers, emphasizing consistency and accountability. Since their focus is on others, social considerations are always in their thoughts. Personal reciprocity in all relationships is paramount. Like STs, they hear and value the conscience of principle as they attempt to fulfill the expectations of their community.

SFs tend to have traditional values that are demonstrated in personal, practical, and tangible ways. From this conventional framework, they will offer concrete support to make families, communities, and institutions functional in terms of service to people. Their ethical evaluations are not likely to be framed in abstract reasoning or overarching systems but rather in more palpable sources such as sayings or stories. Because of their reliance on Sensing, they are attuned to present problems, observing how others are doing by watching their body language or facial expressions. Because of their reliance on Feeling, they are strongly motivated to care for the immediate problems of people. In conclusion, SF morality is best at attending to the practical needs of individuals. They practice doing what's right through care to others.

An SF Ethical Theory: W. D. Ross's *Prima Facie* Duties. Scottish philosopher W. D. Ross represents a development in the Kantian tradition. Ross is committed to a nonconsequentialist approach to ethics, assigning importance to the notion of duty. Unlike Kant, however, he does not understand duty to be an absolute imperative. Kant's ethical stance cannot resolve a commitment to two universal but conflicting imperatives. Kant gives no remedy for which imperative is to take precedence over the other. For example, should a person lie if lying will save the life of someone in mortal danger? Kant argues that one should not lie under any circumstances even if it might result (later) in someone's death. (Kant is unwilling to allow for exceptions; his imperatives are absolute.) Ross, however, argues that a distinction should be made between actual duty and conditional duty. What one actually ought to do or what is actually right can be derived from rules that permit certain exceptions. This he calls "the personal character of duty." Feeling, with its personal impressions, overrides Thinking in this ethical equation. Thus, one's actual duty (lying to preserve human life) might entail the breaking of a conditional duty (never tell a lie). Conditional duties are those which bear *prima facie,* or "at first glance" obligation. They can be suspended, though rarely are, as one evaluates the situation from a personal standpoint. This "personal character" (F) determines the actual duty. Ross, then, is not obligated to absolute duties, but to the evaluation of different competing duties. This pluralistic approach toward duty seems fairer than Kant's unconditional duty.[3]

Ross makes a number of important contributions we should consider when making ethical decisions.

1) **He takes into consideration the complexity of concrete situations in which we must act (S).** Against the consequentialists (N), he insists that the circumstances we face are far too complex to reduce our decisions to only one criterion for determining our behavior—namely, "Does it have good results?"

2) **He takes into consideration the personal nature of our decisions (F).** He claims that our judgments about right and wrong are almost always tentative rather than certain. We cannot have objective, certain knowledge (T). Instead, we must realize that there are honest differences of opinion between people of good morals regarding what should be done in a certain situation. This is the "personal character of duty" or subjective thinking (F).

Ross has been criticized for his logical inconsistency regarding which duties take precedence (T). He does not provide a consistent and universal principle by which one can determine which duties ought to be placed first whenever conflicts arise. Ross admits as much saying, "For the estimation of the comparative stringency of these *prima facie* obligations no general rules can, so far as I can see, be laid down" (Ross, p. 41). Such inconsistency, at times, seems to make him appear a consequentialist, a position he opposes.

How would Ross respond? A city council member promises her fourteen-year-old daughter that she will attend her daughter's basketball game at 3:30 in the afternoon. The council member has an important council meeting that is scheduled to end at 3:15. This will give her just enough time to get to the game for tip-off. The meeting goes later than anticipated, however, due to a heated debate regarding the allocation of some $100,000. The councilwoman favors releasing the money for immediate emergency aid to flood victims in the community. Other council members favor asking the state and national government for assistance. In this later proposal it might be weeks or months before the money materializes. The vote on the issue will be close. Should she miss her daughter's game in order to make sure these needy families receive immediate assistance?

Ross writes that: ". . . there are special obligations arising from acts the very intention of which, when they were done, was to put us under such an obligation" (p. 27). These are called "promises." A promise is a promise and not to be treated lightly. While the city councilwoman can do a great amount of good for the flood victims by breaking her promise to her daughter, Ross does not think that a mathematical formula that weighs overall results has the final say. Yet neither does Ross agree with Kant that one should never break a promise. While a promise seems to be, in principle, our inviolate duty "in actual experience [it is] compounded together in highly complex ways" (p. 27). The case study above presents such complexity. For Ross, "no act is ever, in virtue of falling under some general description, necessarily actually right; its rightness depends on its whole nature and not on any element in it" (p. 33). Ross believes that there are times when one is "justified in breaking, and indeed morally obliged to break, a promise in order to relieve some one's distress . . ." (p. 28). Unlike Kant who would argue categorically that the council-woman should keep her promise to her daughter and unlike J. S. Mill (see forthcoming NT section) who would argue categorically that the greater good would be to break the promise, Ross believes "we come in the long run, after consideration, to think one duty more pressing than the other, but we do not feel certain that it is so" (pp. 30–31). Ross might not provide a definitive moral solution for this case.

SF RULE OF THUMB

SF morality with its conscience of principle answers the question "What should I do?" with "Do the right thing" so that your duty is most appropriately met (S). SF morality answers "How should I decide?" with "Use your heart" subjectively and personally (F).

Part II:

The Conscience of Potential (N): Seeking the Good

Intuitive types, with their focus on the future, take an ethical stance of "seeking the good," thereby expressing a conscience of potential. Their conscience tells them what they should do so that things will turn out well. The formal study of this phenomenon is known as teleology. Teleology is the study of purposeful development toward a final end. Teleological ethical theories are "goal-oriented"; their focus is on the future. These theories suggest that the final appeal must be to the comparative amount of good produced, or to the comparative balance of good over evil. The good of an action is dependent on the good it brings about. One asks, "Are things better than before the action took place?" The maxim often repeated in basketball circles, "no harm, no foul," is an example of a teleological approach. If the act (insignificant contact during play) produces no harm, then perhaps the greater good (a well-played game with little interference from the referees) will result. These theories, therefore, focus on evaluating the hypothetical future consequences of the act (N) rather than the present correctness of the concrete action (S). The conscience given to Intuitive types is a conscience of potential.

An example of a teleological approach to ethics is given in the early chapters of The Gospel of Mark as Jesus of Nazareth begins his itinerant ministry. After Jesus is baptized, he comes into Galilee preaching the "gospel of the kingdom of God." As his fame spreads, he is confronted by religious authorities who oppose his way of doing things. Mark points this out in several controversy stories in which Jesus breaks the rules of his religion and culture, and is criticized for such things as eating with "tax collectors and sinners," eating on regular fast days, and healing on the Sabbath. On one occasion, Mark records that Jesus and his disciples are walking through a corn field on the Sabbath and that his disciples are plucking and eating the ears of corn as they pass. This is a violation of Jewish law and, in fact, breaks the fourth of the Ten Commandments: "Honor the Sabbath and

Keep it Holy." When the Pharisees criticize Jesus, saying that his disciples are breaking the law, Jesus responds in Mark 2:25–28b saying,

> "Have you never read what David did when he and his companions were hungry and in need of food? He entered the house of God, when Abiathar was high priest, and ate the bread of the Presence, which it is not lawful for any but the priests to eat, and he gave some to his companions." Then he said to them, "The Sabbath was made for humankind, and not humankind for the Sabbath. . . ." (NRSV)

Jesus gives a teleological argument here by saying that it is morally acceptable for his disciples to break the Jewish religious law since they are famished. In the same way, King David of the Old Testament violated religious law in order to feed his companions. Jesus' famous expression, "The Sabbath was made for humankind, and not humankind for the Sabbath," is a summary of his ethical approach: laws are made for the good of people. If following the law has a good result then we should follow it; if breaking the law has a good result then, perhaps, we should break it. What matters most is the end result of one's actions (feeding the hungry) and not the action itself (violating the Sabbath code). This is the conscience of potential.

Intuitive types are likely to find value in teleological approaches since they are adept at considering possibilities and eventualities. They project into the future and predict outcomes. Intuition combined with Thinking (NT) or with Feeling (NF) is likely to produce distinctive ways of morally evaluating future events.

NT Justice

The greatest good for the greatest number.

Summary: Seeking the good consistently.
Best at: Focusing on broad, impersonal concepts and issues; analyzing complex, objective situations.

Moral Considerations of the NT Type. The NT moral stance is usually grounded in a unifying vision that organizes all of life into a comprehensive whole. The intuitive ability to envision is characteristic of NTs who bring a global perspective to their ethical evaluations. Mentally mapping the whole gives NTs the assurance they need to provide meaning and substance to their everyday decision making. Directly engaging life's problems without first conceptualizing them may be uncomfortable for NTs. They seek, in this way, to find clarity and precision in the complexity of daily decisions. In linking Thinking with their big picture perspective from Intuition, they demand intellectual rigor and structural integrity in formulating and expressing ideas. In moral decision making, the NT universal perspective seeks justice and equity for the larger community.

With their ability to see the big picture and project into the future, NTs are often valued by institutions and communities as visionaries. NTs enjoy the objective exchange of intellectual ideas and are eager to try their own theories against others. Such exchange may provide a fertilizing agent for NTs in their quest for synthesis. Their dedication to clear thinking and to results that benefit the whole allow them to become instigators for necessary improvements in communities. NTs attend to the conscience of potential as they seek the good for humankind.

NTs are the most likely types to be instigators of change in the world. They are good critics since they are usually proficient at impersonally analyzing situations. If they are unsatisfied with the status quo, they may be quick to disparage an imperfect system. If their myopia for system integrity becomes stringent and overbearing, others may see them as obstinate or compulsive. Their consistency, however, enhances their chances of effecting change. NT morality is best at analyzing complex, objective situations by focusing on broad, impersonal concepts and issues. In short, NT morality seeks the good with logical coherence to a vision.

An NT Ethical Theory: J. S. Mill's Utilitarianism. The liberal English philosopher John Stuart Mill (1806–1873) was one of the most influential founders of utilitarianism as an ethical theory. Utilitarianism maintains that the morality of an action is to be determined solely through an assessment of its consequences (N). It demands that we consider the impact of the consequences on everyone affected by the matter under consideration (T). The morally right action, the one that we ought to perform, is the one that produces the greatest overall positive consequences for everyone. Historically, utilitarians have taken pleasure (Jeremy Bentham) and happiness (J. S. Mill) as the measure of consequences. More recent theorists have turned either to higher ("ideal") goods (G. E. Moore) or to preferences (K. J. Arrow) as the measuring stick. Utilitarians claim that, in any given situation, we must as best as we can (1) determine the consequences (N) of the various courses of action available, (2) specify and analyze the positives and negatives (T) associated with each alternative, and (3) perform the deed that results in the greatest total amount of good over evil.

The contributions of a utilitarian approach to ethics are significant.

1) **Consequences are important (N).** Utilitarians remind us that "seeking the good" in every circumstance is as significant as "doing the right." They constantly evaluate who will be harmed or helped as a result of their decisions. They remind us that our choices have actual effects on society.

2) **Impartiality (T).** Utilitarians, since they are committed to bringing about the greatest benefit to the greatest number of people, do not make exceptions for individuals, themselves included. This objectivity achieved through rational analysis is characteristic of our U.S. justice system, symbolized by lady justice, blindfolded, holding a scale in one hand and a sword in the other. Her blindfold insures that Feeling is kept in check.

3) **Consistency (T).** If one applies a utilitarian principle to all ethical decisions (e.g., perform the act that will produce the greatest overall good) one's decisions will be uniform and predictable. The consistent action of a nation's citizenry is essential to the maintenance of civil society.

Like all theories, utilitarianism has its weaknesses.

1) **Utilitarianism has a tendency toward numerical evaluation.** Some things cannot be assigned numerical value. For example, consider a developing country where a small percentage of the children are prostitutes. Each year thousands of wealthy tourists from foreign countries spend their vacations there, in part because of easy access to sexual experiences. The tourism industry leads this small country in revenue produced. Tourism provides jobs for a large segment of the population with employment in hotels, airports, restaurants, transportation, game parks, shops, etc. While child prostitution helps to attract foreign money to their country, the child prostitutes themselves do not benefit from prostitution. Many of these children, in fact, experience physical trauma, disease, and early death in the marketing of their bodies. A utilitarian might logically argue that child prostitution should be continued in the country since the benefits to the many easily outweigh the pain of the few. This kind of logic, however, seems grossly immoral.

2) **Lack of attention to Feeling.** While utilitarianism gives some weight to human feelings (e.g., Mill's happiness or

Bentham's pleasure), the evaluation seems to be based on what value these feelings have for their overall social utility. The feelings and the human relationships engendered by these feelings do not seem to be valued except as they promote something else. Such bifurcation robs us of our moral sentiments and perhaps even of our conscience.

3) **Utilitarianism tends to ignore the limits of human responsibility.** In the television series "Marshall Dillon," Matt Dillon is sometimes required, for the good of Dodge City, to shoot villains. His reaction after killing a man is always matter-of-fact and routine. He often responds with: "Well I hated to do it but I had to; I didn't have any choice, he pulled a gun." While one cannot deny that shooting a villain may be the best choice for the overall good of society, Marshall Dillon does not attach any special weight to the fact that he is the one who pulls the trigger. It's just his job! What utilitarianism misses is the fact that human beings bear an intimate relationship to their own actions regardless of whatever good or bad consequences follow.

4) **The limits of our reasoning ability.** Utilitarians make decisions based on rational predictions about what will occur in the future. Yet our abilities to do this are limited since we cannot be certain what will happen. The nature of the world is that it is unpredictable and we cannot with any certainty know how things will turn out.

How would J. S. Mill respond? You enter a burning building to discover two people lying unconscious on the floor. One is your own father and the other is a medical genius who has just discovered a cure for cancer. Who do you carry out of the building and who do you leave to die?

The utilitarian calculus demands that you carry out the medical genius. Mill writes: "The creed which accepts as the foundation of morals 'utility' or the 'greatest happiness principle' holds that actions are right in proportion as they tend to promote happiness; wrong as they tend to produce the reverse of happiness" (p. 10). If the medical genius is saved, millions of people benefit and much human suffering will be alleviated. Since this is the greater good, your father must remain behind.

NT RULE OF THUMB

NT morality with its conscience of potential answers the question "What should I do?" with "Seek the good" consistently (N). NT morality answers "How should I decide?" with "Use your head" objectively and impersonally (T).

NF Compassion

You shall love your neighbor as yourself.
— MARK 12:31

Summary: Seeking the good for others.
Best at: Promoting harmony in complex interpersonal situations; making institutions and laws responsive to people.

Moral Considerations of the NF Type. NFs tend to be the most idealistic of the four types, combining a global vision with a feeling for the well-being of other people. This commitment sometimes takes an unconventional moral stance that may at times be impractical and overreaching, yet NF inspiration can be the catalyst for important social change. NFs are at home on the global field, in touch with the trends and patterns existing in the society at large. Such Intuitive perception when combined with Feeling produces values that focus on possibilities, on future benefits for people. Compassionate idealism characterizes the moral commitments of many NFs.

NFs are often excellent spokespersons for moral causes since they combine an intuitive tendency for myth and symbol with an ability to empathize with the plight of those in need. In this way they can often energize a cause by tapping into the collective unconscious in ways that motivate others to action. NFs tend to need affirmation from others and work best when they know they are trusted and valued. Even so, NFs, with their conscience of potential, can stand alone or against the conventional perspective if the situation demands it.

NF morality, which strives for equanimity and harmony, does not necessarily reconcile conflicting values in order for arguments to be logically consistent. Instead, they have a tendency to appreciate a wide variety of perspectives and are, thus, highly tolerant of differing moral positions. NFs can suspend their own beliefs and appreciate, or even affirm, other positions without having a need to reconcile such ambiguity. They are able to do this because of their intense desire for social harmony and conflict avoidance. NFs are perhaps the most pliable of the groups and have a need to please others (F). Because of this, they sometimes have a difficult time taking criticism. NFs tend to be seekers, always looking for new insights and new paths to explore. This is in large part due to their ability to see possibilities. Such vision causes them to live in the future rather than in the here-and-now. For that reason, others may see NFs as unstable or irresolute, even reckless. In conclusion, the NF contribution to ethics lies in the desire to promote peace and harmony in complex interpersonal situations and in making institutions and laws responsive to people. In this way, NFs tend to seek the good for others.

An NF Ethical Theory: Joseph Fletcher's Situation Ethics.
Joseph Fletcher's *Situation Ethic: The New Morality* (1967) is an important work in ethical theory from a Christian perspective.[4] As a teleological ethical stance, situation ethics takes into account particular actions and circumstances. No two situations are treated the same; each is viewed as a unique event. The decisions that are made cannot be absolutized but are determined to be appropriate for a given set of circumstances. Rules may guide but they cannot determine action. In determining right from wrong,

only the consequences (N) and the behavior which affects the specific situations of the individuals involved (F) are significant. No predetermined rules (S) can be applied when faced with a moral dilemma. No act is intrinsically good or evil. Any action, given the right circumstances, might be ethically prudent. According to Fletcher, "Only one thing is intrinsically good, namely love: nothing else at all" (p. 68). One is obliged to make all decisions on the basis of love. In answering the question of whether an action was right or wrong one asks: "Did you act in love?" This is an NF question which means: "Did you intend to bring (N) good or ill to the human situation (F)?"

Situation ethics makes important contributions to ethical theory. Fletcher writes: "In the coalition the hedonistic calculus becomes the agapeic [selfless love] calculus, the greatest amount of neighbor welfare for the largest number of neighbors possible" (p. 95). This formula points to two NF values.

1) **The importance of responsibility for one's actions (N).** Fletcher issues a call to be aware that every decision changes outcomes. In this way, situation ethics places an enormous burden on the individual as an actor in events. A person cannot excuse himself from what he says or does on the basis of simply following a predetermined set of rules. This is a call to radical responsibility since the decisions may, at times, run counter to the collective conscience and conventional morality. Fletcher admits that this responsibility is difficult for most people to sustain.

2) **The need to empathize with fellow human beings (F).** Fletcher's *agapeism* places the welfare of people above all other considerations. He asks us to consider our neighbor's plight since, in the end, people are what matter most. He writes that "love wears blinders, sees only the neighbor *there*" (p. 97).

There are several weaknesses to this theory.

1) **Situation ethics has a relativistic bent.** Fletcher proposes that we look at each situation in an entirely unique way. But is this humanly possible? Can one ignore moral princi-

ples that have been practiced and upheld with good reason over time? And aren't some actions always morally wrong, every time?

2) **Does *agapeism* work in larger social contexts?** While it may be possible to show love to my neighbor who wrongs me, how does society at large show love to hardened criminals? Is love really more important than justice in the larger context? Can love be the primary motive of the judge or the police officer who must distribute justice?

3) **Isn't this way of doing ethics possible only for a few since it places such a large responsibility on the actor?** Even if we eliminate children and adolescents, do many mature adults ever reach the moral stage that would allow them to make such unilateral decisions? Is Fletcher asking humans to play God?

How would Fletcher respond? A small neighborhood merchant is approached by three large men who ask if he has seen a local resident named John Smith. The merchant is actually a friend of John Smith and knows where John Smith is at that very moment. The three men, on the other hand, are known racketeers and out to possibly harm his friend. In order to protect his friend the merchant tells a lie saying, "I haven't seen Mr. Smith in weeks."

Fletcher writes:

> If a lie is told unlovingly it is wrong, evil; if it is told in love it is good, right. Kant's legalism produced a "universal"— that a lie is always wrong. But what if you have to tell a lie to keep a promised secret? Maybe you lie, and if so, good for you if you follow love's lead. Paul's "speaking the truth in love" (Eph. 4:15) illuminates the point; we are to tell the truth for love's sake, not for its own sake. If love vetoes the truth, so be it. Right and wrong, good and bad, are things that *happen* to what we say and do, whether they are "veracious" or not, depending upon how much love is served in the situation. The merchant chose to do a good thing, not an excusably bad thing. Love made it good. *The situationist holds that whatever is the most loving thing in the situation is the right and good thing.* (p. 65)

NF RULE OF THUMB

NF morality with its conscience of potential answers the question "What should I do?" with "Seek the good" for others (N). NF morality answers "How should I decide?" with "Use your heart" subjectively and personally (F).

Summary

Type theory suggests that STs, SFs, NTs, and NFs arrive at ethical decisions by different routes. The functions of the given (Sensation or Intuition) are likely to determine whether a person approaches ethical decision making from a deontological (duty-oriented) or teleological (goal-oriented) perspective. Sensing types are likely to value deontological approaches which focus on the act rather than the value that an act brings into existence. Deontological approaches answer the question "What should I do?" with "Do the right thing." This is the conscience of principle. Intuitive types are likely to value teleological approaches which focus on the value an act brings into existence rather than the act itself. Teleological approaches answer the question "What should I do?" with "Seek the good." This is the conscience of potential.

The functions of option (Thinking and Feeling) are likely to determine whether a person uses the head or the heart in answering the question "How should I decide?" The deontological theories of Immanuel Kant and W. D. Ross resonate with ST and SF perspectives while the teleological theories of J. S. Mill and Joseph Fletcher correspond to NT and NF perspectives. While these theories are natural starting points for the corresponding types, a well balanced decision making process should consider both functions of the given and both functions of option. Jung suggests that a dialectic in which each function is allowed its distinctive voice is necessary in order for a person to become fully aware in a moral sense. Chapter 5 explores this dialectical approach to ethical decision making.

Chapter Five

THE ULTIMATE PURPOSE IN STUDYING ETHICS IS NOT AS IT IS IN OTHER INQUIRIES, THE ATTAINMENT OF THEORETICAL KNOWLEDGE; WE ARE NOT CONDUCTING THIS INQUIRY IN ORDER TO KNOW WHAT VIRTUE IS, BUT IN ORDER TO BECOME GOOD, ELSE THERE WOULD BE NO ADVANTAGE IN STUDYING IT.

— ARISTOTLE

Putting It All Together

A Jungian Perspective

Type theory assumes we have an innate way of doing ethics based on our typological strengths. While most of us make ethical decisions in a habitual way, we may not be conscious of this process. Chapter 4 connects typology to ethical theories in part to give philosophical substance and depth to these habitual patterns at work in decision making. Such study enhances our ability to make conscious our moral decisions. Knowing how we weigh and value issues is of great importance and allows us to make better decisions.

C. G. Jung argues that we use all four functions (S, N, T, and F) but in different capacities and degrees. We each have a dominant function which we use most of the time and an auxiliary function which compliments and gives balance to the dominant function. The tertiary and inferior functions are usually neglected and rarely used. One of the primary tasks in the first half of life, according to Jung, is development of the ego. This is accomplished in part through the successful development of the dominant and auxiliary functions. The tertiary and inferior functions often remain dormant and unconscious during early years. Jung argues, however, that in order to "individuate" or become whole we must develop these third and fourth functions. This is the task of the second half of life.

It follows then that the morally mature person uses all four functions.[1] A Jungian perspective, modeled on the individuation process, assumes that an individual's ethical stance matches his or her dominant and auxiliary functions. Thus, it would be natural for an NT to be a utilitarian, an NF to be a situationist, etc. Since, however, all ethical theories have strengths and weaknesses,

Jungian psychology suggests that the tertiary and inferior functions must also be consulted in order for ethical wholeness to result. Thus an NT utilitarian who takes the time to consults his SF functions gains an important and perhaps even missing moral component. An NF situationist who checks her moral commitments against an ST argument can find her own stance challenged and strengthened.

The Ethical Types Mandala (figure 2) expresses the moral wholeness that can be sought by each of us. A mandala is a symbol of oneness, totality, or integration. Typically, it is a circle enclosing a square and is used for meditative visualization among various religious traditions. While expressing unity, the alternating squares within are meant to depict the dualistic but complementary principles of the universe.

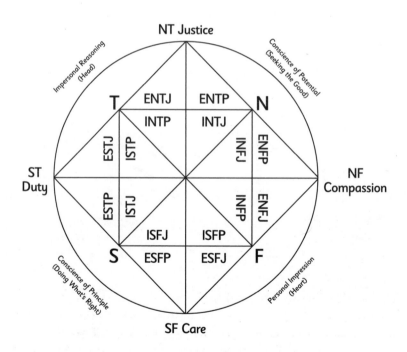

Figure 2 Ethical Types Mandala

The Ethical Types Mandala is an alternative way of showing relationships between the sixteen types.[2] Typical diagrams employed in MBTI publications are rectangular. In using a circle, relationships between the types can be envisioned in more fluid and interacting ways. The key aspect of the mandala is the position of the four function types arranged along the axes of the circle and across from their opposite: NT Justice is opposite SF Care; ST Duty is opposite NF Compassion. Within the circle are four squares. Each square is composed of four types that share dominant/auxiliary functions. For example, in the top NT square are located ENTJ, ENTP, INTP, and INTJ. One can readily see, therefore, which types are closely related and which types are dissimilar. Through this arrangement, one can also observe what components of ethical decision making the various types hold in common. For example, the ST Duty quadrant has in common with the SF Care quadrant the Sensing types' conscience of principle, which aims to "do what's right." The ST Duty quadrant has in common with the NT Justice quadrant the tendency of Thinking types to use impersonal reasoning in moral deliberations. One can also observe opposites at work in the mandala. For example, the INFJ space is positioned to show variance with the ESTP space, the ESFJ space with the INTP space, etc.

Again, the Jungian charge is that one masters a particular way, then later "rounds out" the perspective by considering polar perspectives. Such is the way of moral integrity.

Step by Step

The following descriptions provide a summary of each type group's corresponding ethical theory including a step-by-step approach to the particular moral stance. Each description concludes with questions for each particular type. These questions are designed to force one to consider the moral dimensions of the tertiary and inferior functions. The final aim is a dialectic between the functions so that moral integration is possible.

ST Duty

Summary: Doing the right thing consistently.
Ethical Theory: Immanuel Kant's Categorical Imperative.
Approach: Deontological theories maintain that the morality of an action is to be determined solely by the act itself rather than the value it brings into existence (S). Kantian ethics call us to follow unambiguous, objective, universal principles determined by reason (T).
The bottom line: The morally right action is the one done out of duty as prescribed by a universal principle.

STEPS:

1. What should I do? The conscience of principle says "Do what's right."

By using your Sensing perception determine what is the right thing to do in this situation. In doing so, consider: **(a)** What happened or what is happening? Identify the relevant facts (who, what, when, where, and how). Pay particular attention to pre-scribed rules and duties (legal, corporate, religious, personal, moral). **(b)** What is at stake? What is the main ethical issue in this situation?

2. How should I decide? Use your head.

By using your Thinking judgment determine what is just. What should happen in order for you to perform your moral duty? Consider: **(a)** an impersonal principle of duty that will be applied impartially and consistently in every situation; **(b)** a logical syllogism or syllogisms[3] which support the argument.

3. A dialectic with the NF functions.

After making a decision based on the ST model, reexamine your commitment by asking the following question: What are the possible consequences of my action (N) on the people involved in this situation (F)?

SF Care

Summary: Doing the right thing by serving others.
Ethical Theory: W. D. Ross's *Prima Facie* Duties.
Basic Approach: Deontological theories maintain that the morality of an action is to be determined solely by the act itself rather than the value it brings into existence (S). Ross suggests that we use common sense to determine our appropriate duty to people served (F).
The bottom line: The morally right action is the one done out of respect for duties that guide but do not determine personal decisions of care.

STEPS:

1. What should I do? The conscience of principle says "Do what's right."

By using your Sensing perception determine what is the right thing to do in this situation. In doing so, consider: **(a)** What happened or what is happening? Identify the relevant facts (who, what, when, where, and how). Pay particular attention to pre-scribed rules and responsibilities (legal, corporate, religious, personal, moral). **(b)** What is at stake? What is the main ethical issue in this situation?

2. How should I decide? Use your heart.

By using your Feeling judgment determine the most caring response. Of the various rules and duties expounded above what single rule or duty should be followed in order that the welfare of the people involved is placed above all else? What is lost and gained in human terms by following this duty above all others?

3. A dialectic with the NT functions.

After making a decision based on the SF model, reexamine your commitment by asking the following question: What will be the consequences of my action to the society at large (N) if they are habitual and done consistently (T) over a long period of time?

NT Justice

Summary: Seeking the good consistently.

Ethical theory: J. S. Mill's Utilitarianism.

Basic approach: Teleological theories maintain that the morality of an action is to be determined solely through an assessment of its consequences (N). Utilitarian theories commit us to consider the impact of the consequences on everyone affected by the matter under consideration (T).

The bottom line: The morally right action is the one that produces the greatest overall positive consequences for a just society.

STEPS:

1. What should I do? The conscience of potential says "Seek the good."

By using your Intuitive perception determine what should happen to bring about a good result in this situation. In doing so, consider: **(a)** What is at stake? What is the *main* ethical issue at stake and why is it important? How is this issue similar to other issues? Sort out important issues from trivial. **(b)** What could happen? Determine the consequences of the various courses of action available. How is this situation similar to other situations?

2. How should I decide? Use your head.

By using your Thinking judgment determine what is just. Of the possibilities explored what should occur in order for justice to be served? Consider: **(a)** an impersonal principle of justice that will be applied impartially and consistently in every situation. **(b)** a logical syllogism or syllogisms which support the argument.

3. A dialectic with the SF functions.

After making a decision based on the NT model, reexamine your commitment by asking the following question: How does the specific action that I take (S) demonstrate personal faithfulness to those individuals with whom I have a relationship (F)?

NF Compassion

Summary: Seeking the good for others.
Ethical Theory: Joseph Fletcher's Situation Ethics.
Basic Approach: Teleological theories maintain that the morality of an action is to be determined solely through an assessment of its consequences (N). Situationism considers the impact that universal principles have on the particular people involved (F).
The bottom line: The morally right action is the one that produces the greatest overall positive consequences for the welfare of individuals in that particular situation.

STEPS:

1. What should I do? The conscience of potential says "Seek the good."

By using your Intuitive perception determine what should happen to bring about a good result in this situation. In doing so, consider: **(a)** What is at stake? What is the *main* ethical issue in this case and why is it important? How is this issue similar to other issues? Sort out important issues from trivial. **(b)** What could happen? Determine the consequences of the various courses of action available. How is this situation similar to other situations?

2. How should I decide? Use your heart.

By using your Feeling judgment determine the most caring response. Of the possibilities explored what should happen in order that the welfare of the people involved is placed above all else? What is lost and gained in human terms? What do you intend to bring about by your actions?

3. A dialectic with the ST functions.

After making a decision based on the NF model, reexamine your commitment by asking the following question: Am I willing to allow for the specific action which I take (S) to be made public and codified (T) for the general usage?

A Disclaimer

Jung said that "theories are the very devil." While simplification of any process is helpful especially in the learning stages of an activity, it is important to remember that the master of a craft always transcends the codification of the process. Athletes, musicians, writers sometimes violate or extend the rules of their craft in the creative endeavor. The step-by-step process above is designed to assist you in becoming more conscious of how you make moral decisions. Knowing one's strengths and weaknesses is necessary in the mastery of the moral craft. Jung reminds us to be humble in this effort since there is always an equal and opposite perspective at work in life's complications. He writes, "That is what makes the integration of the unconscious so difficult: we have to learn to think in antinomies, constantly bearing in mind that every truth turns into an antinomy if it is thought out to the end" (p. 14).

Chapter Six

**I LEARNED ALL I KNOW
ABOUT ETHICS IN SPORTS.**

— ALBERT CAMUS

Putting Theory to Practice

Consider a Case Study: The "Good" Foul

My name is Thomas Browne. I was asked to substitute as the ninth grade boy's basketball coach for the Hewitt Catholic High School. Coach McClain, the normal coach, contracted pneumonia and was unable to coach during the month of February. As I had recently retired from public teaching and had some free time on my hands, the principal asked me to take over the team during the coach's absence. I had coached a tenth grade team over twenty years ago in Miami, Florida and was a big basketball fan.

The team's record was 7–4 when I took over. Over the four weeks that I coached, we won two games and lost six. While our record was not great, I was proud of the chance to teach the guys something about good sportsmanship.

Maybe I'm from the "old school" but I was concerned when I took over about some of the questionable tactics that Coach McClain had taught them. Perhaps this was excusable because of his age; Coach McClain was only twenty-three years old. The main issue had to do with deliberately fouling an opponent.

Coach McClain was teaching his players two things that I disagreed with completely. First, he was teaching one of his players how to hold his opponent so that the referee would not see it. He taught this technique to Brandon, the team's best post player. He taught Brandon to half front his opponent and hook his arm underneath his opponent's arm. This made it more difficult for the opponent to catch a pass. Coach McClain was teaching Brandon to do this both intentionally and covertly. I believed this was a deliberate violation of the rules of the game and, therefore, cheating.

Second, Coach McClain was doing something that it seems many people do these days but is wrong as well. At the end of a game, if his team was behind, he would tell his players to deliberately foul the other team's poorest free throw shooter. This, as everyone knows, is the so-called "good" foul. This strategy apparently helped the team win three close games in January against stronger opponents. I heard the boys bragging and laughing about how it happened. I'm sorry, but just because everyone does it doesn't make it right. Cheating is cheating. Intentionally holding is not a part of the game of basketball. It is against the rules. How can we teach our youth that it's OK to break a rule for their own self-interest on the basketball court but not to speed when late for an appointment or steal if they want a new stereo? This is morally inconsistent. Right is right and wrong is wrong.

After I realized what was going on, I set up an appointment with the principal. Without going into details, I told him that I would not allow the boys to deliberately break the rules in order to gain an advantage. The principal agreed with my position. Over the course of those four weeks that I coached the team, I did not allow this kind of cheating. The boys all complained about it, as did some of the parents, but that's the way I saw it. We did lose several close games. I was disappointed that in one of those games, the opposing coach told his players to foul our poorest free throw shooter, Scott, who ended up missing his free throws. Scott was humiliated after this loss. I would hate to have cheated in order to win a game.[1]

Typological Analyses

What do you think? Did the interim coach, Mr. Browne, do the right thing? Did he try to do the best for all involved in this case? Four differing perspectives are presented below which correspond to the ST, SF, NT, and NF positions. These examples serve to show how different types might approach the moral dilemma in the case study: The "Good" Foul.

ST Duty

1. What should I do? Determine what is the right thing to do by considering:

(S) What happened? The basic facts of this case are as follows: An elderly gentleman, Mr. Browne, who had limited basketball experience, was asked to substitute for a parochial school's ninth grade basketball team for one month. He was presumably unpaid for this and was probably selected because no one else would do it. The team he coached was not particularly talented but they had done well before he took over with a record of 7–4, even beating some teams that were stronger than them. It appears that in some close games, their slight margin of victory was due to some questionable strategy by the coach, Mr. McClain. The substitute coach, Mr. Browne, believed this strategy to be cheating. Mr. Browne spoke to the principal about this but did not reveal the details about what he believed the cheating to be. During the four weeks that Mr. Browne coached, he would not allow the boys to use this strategy. All of the boys and some of the parents did not like this move. The team lost most of its games. In one game, they apparently lost because the opposing coach employed the strategy that Mr. Browne had forbidden his players to use. Mr. Browne believed that he had taught the boys a lesson in good sportsmanship.

In coming to some resolution regarding the morally correct thing to do in this case, it is important to consider the rules of basketball. There are basically three kinds of rules that operate to guarantee that a good game is played. The first are called prescriptive rules. Prescriptive rules tell you what you must do to play basketball. You must, for example, dribble or pass to advance the ball; you cannot run down the court with the ball. The second kind of rules are called tactics. Tactics are rules that allow one to play the game well. For example, it is good strategy to have the player who can jump the highest to jump center at the start of the game. Tactical rules that are within the prescribed rules are allowed; tactics that are outside of the prescribed rules are, of course, not allowed and labeled as cheating. The third kind of rules are called proscriptions. Proscriptions are direct attempts to reduce or eliminate certain actions so that players face the same test. Proscriptions eliminate certain kinds of tactics like stalling the ball, goal tending, holding, tripping, etc. In the case being considered, there are two kinds of tactics being questioned. In both examples, there is a deliberate violation of the prescribed rules of the game. Both examples given consider a player who holds (or fouls) another player. Holding is not allowed by the rules of basketball. There is a difference, however, in the two examples. In the first, where the defensive player holds the offensive pivot to prevent the pass, the player intends to deceive the referee. In other words, he wants to break the rule and not pay the penalty. In the second, there is no intent to deceive. The player willingly pays the penalty.[2]

(S) **What is at stake?** The *main* ethical issue in this case is: Were Coach McClain's tactics cheating? How should the game be played from a moral point of view? I will restrict my arguments to this basic point and seek to prove that the interim coach, Mr. Browne, was correct in his assessment of the first and second rules violations.

2. How should I decide? Determine what is just by considering:

(T) **An impersonal principle of duty.** Though we are talking about the rules of basketball, it is important to consider that these rules are reflections of more universal laws that should govern human behavior. Consider the Golden Rule: "Do unto others as you would have them do unto you." If I am allowed to do something, then everyone else should be allowed to do it as well. I can't make an exception for myself. The rules of basketball are created so that a good sports contest can be played. Deliberately violating the rules of the game destroys the agreed-upon mutual test of the players. If a player breaks the rules of the game to gain an advantage and does not expect the same advantage to be given to his opponent, then that is wrong; it is cheating.

(T) A syllogism. In both situations we have a coach who is teaching his players to deliberately violate the rules. This is being done in a tactical way in order to gain an advantage. From a logical point of view, to violate the rules deliberately is to destroy the good sports contest. In fact, a player who deliberately breaks the rules is no longer playing that game. Neither of these tactics should be allowed based on the following syllogism: (1) the rules of basketball are designed to make it a good sports contest; (2) players and coaches tacitly agree when they decide to compete that they will follow the rules of the game; therefore, (3) intentional rules violations are never appropriate.

Let's also look at the two types of fouls separately. First, a player knowingly and intentionally violates a rule to gain an advantage, but skillfully attempts to do so while avoiding a penalty. In addition to the argument above, I would further clarify this type of rules violation by making the following points: (1) the skills being tested in a basketball game are not skills in how to deceive the referee; (2) the advantage gained in holding an opponent is based on deceiving the referee; therefore, (3) holding your opponent is inappropriate in basketball since it changes the kind of skills being evaluated in the sport. The bottom line is this: The good sports contest in basketball is one in which both opponents are evaluated based on constitutive rules (which do not involve deception). The maxim we are attempting to follow here is "Do unto others as you would have them do unto you." In this situation, if my action (i.e., deceptively holding an opponent) became universal (that is accepted within the rules of basketball), I would lose the advantage I had in doing it in the first place. In other words, the only reason for employing this strategy is that it is outside of the rules and gives an unfair advantage. Since you cannot apply our universal maxim to this case, it should not be allowed.

Second, a player knowingly violates a rule but expects and willingly accepts the penalty. The "good" foul occurs when a defensive player fouls an offensive player who is dribbling for an easy lay up shot, forcing him to shoot two free throws. Though the player's intent is different here (i.e., he expects to receive a penalty for his actions), the action is the same. The syllogism I expressed in the paragraph above works for this situation as well. The bottom line is: The "good" foul is intentionally performing skills proscribed by the rules. Some might argue here that the "good" foul is simply a "part of the game" but this is refuted by recent changes in college and professional basketball rules to fix even greater penalties on intentional fouls. It is clear that the "good" foul detracts from the well-played basketball game.

Conclusion. I agree with Mr. Browne's decision. He was right regarding both situations. His Sense perception seems adequate in that he knows the rules of basketball well. His Thinking judgment, however, is suspect. He basically gives no logical arguments for his position. He simply says, "cheating is cheating" without giving careful thought to his position. Had he thought through this logically he could have been more convincing. Perhaps the players and the parents would have come over to his side. As it was, I doubt the players learned much about being good sports.

A dialectic with the NF functions. How is the decision going to affect (N) the people involved in this situation (F)?

The future is complicated by the fact that Mr. Browne is only the interim coach and Mr. McClain is going to return to coach the team. We can only assume that Coach McClain will continue teaching these questionable tactics. If we think about the ethical development of these ninth grade players, we may have to reconsider Mr. Browne's firm and isolated stand. Though I believe he is on the right side of the issue, his position in the long-run may cause moral confusion. Certainly these fourteen-year-olds are being given mixed signals. I must agree that this is something he should have thought about beforehand.

SF Care

1. What should I do? Do the right thing by considering:

(S) What happened? The basic facts of this case are as follows: Mr. Browne, a retired school teacher, was asked to substitute for a Catholic school's ninth grade basketball team. He had limited experience as a coach. The team he took over was not very good but were overachievers and had amassed a respectable 7–4 record, even beating some better squads. They won some close games, in part, because of some heady but questionable strategy by the real coach, Coach McClain. The substitute coach, Mr. Browne, believed this strategy to be cheating. Mr. Browne spoke to the principal about this but did not go into great detail about what was going on. He just told the principal that he would not allow the boys to deliberately break the rules. During the month that Mr. Browne coached, he did not allow the team to use this strategy. All of the boys and some of the parents protested. The team lost most of its games and in one game, they apparently lost because the opposing coach employed the strategy that Mr. Browne would not allow his players to use. Mr. Browne believed that he had taught the boys a lesson in good sportsmanship.

There are some rules and responsibilities involved in this case which we must consider. (1) What is the duty of a coach to the game of basketball? It seems obvious that a coach must teach his players the correct way to play the game. In doing so he must teach them the rules of the game and the appropriate tactics to use during the game. In the case being considered, there are two kinds of tactics being questioned. In both examples, there is a deliberate violation of the prescribed rules of the game. Both examples given consider a player who holds (or fouls) another player. Holding is not allowed by the rules of basketball. (There is a difference, however, in the two examples. In the first, where the defensive player holds the offensive pivot to prevent the pass, the player intends to deceive the referee. In other words, he wants to break the rule and not pay the penalty. In the second, there is no intent to deceive. The player willingly pays the penalty.) (2) Does the responsibility to win take precedence over the responsibility to teach good sportsmanship for a ninth grade coach? (3) What is the duty of an interim coach? Should he change strategy during the middle of the season? If so, what steps should be taken regarding these changes? Was this done? (4) What is the duty of the principal regarding the hiring of coaches? Did the principal know what the interim coach was doing? (5) What is the duty of a coach of a ninth grade team regarding the teaching of morals? Is there any difference in teaching sportsmanship to ninth graders as distinct from college athletes or professional athletes? Is there a limit to gamesmanship, especially in youth sports?

(S) **What is at stake?** There are two main ethical issues in this case: (1) Is deliberately fouling an opponent wrong in ninth grade basketball? (2) Should the interim coach change Coach McClain's strategy regarding deliberately fouling an opponent? In order to make my case, I will discuss the competing duties that a coach has and show that the interim coach was correct in his assessment of the first rules violation but incorrect in his assessment of the second rules violation. I will further show that, beyond his assessment of the moral viability of each situation, he had other responsibilities as an interim coach that he did not fulfill.

2. How should I decide?

(F) **Determine the most caring response.** Let's begin with the first situation—a defensive player deliberately holds an offensive pivot skillfully in order to avoid a penalty. First, is such action to be taught by a ninth grade coach? I think it should not be taught because it is clear that holding violates the written rules of basketball. But the question remains whether there are any unwritten rules allowing for this kind of deceptive holding. Certainly, in the NBA, coaches teach this kind of behavior. It is an unwritten rule that deceiving the referee is a part of the game. An example here would be a "flop," where the defensive player tries to draw a charge. But our situation is not the NBA; our situation is a ninth grade school team. I do not believe that this kind of deceptive practice is expected of a ninth grader. In other words, I don't believe it is a "part of the game" at that level of play. A major duty of a ninth grade coach is to teach respect for the referee. While deceiving the referee may be accepted as "gamesmanship" in the NBA, I do not believe it is appropriate at the ninth grade level. Children at this age cannot so easily compartmentalize life. Teaching kids to deceive authority is not in their moral best interest. Thus, it appears that Coach McClain was teaching a player named Brandon to cheat in this situation. While he has a duty as coach to put his players in the best position to win, this duty should not supersede his duty to teach good sportsmanship.

Second, once the interim coach determined that this was cheating, what should he have done? Here, I do not believe that he handled himself well. An interim coach must realize that he is only there for a short period. Unless he has support from the principal, parents, players, and the real head coach, he may end up causing more problems than he solves by changing strategies in mid-stream. He should have gone first to the head coach and expressed his disapproval of what he believed to be cheating. It is the duty of an interim coach to keep the ship running while the captain is away. Mutiny is not an expectation. In conversations with the head coach and the principal, an agreement might have been reached so that the kids were not taught two different things. To teach two different sets of values to kids can be more damaging than to teach one set of inferior values. Since Coach McClain was only twenty-three years old, it is possible that he could have been guided by the interim and the principal. As it stands, I am not at all sure that the best thing was done for Brandon and the other players. When Coach McClain comes back, will Brandon follow his instructions? Surely Brandon will be confused. Interim Coach Browne failed to realize that he had a limited role to play.

Regarding the second situation: A player fouls a poor free throw shooter toward the end of the game in order to make him shoot free throws. First, is this cheating? I believe it is not because in this situation, fouling is an accepted part of strategy at the ninth grade level. It is a part of the unwritten rules; indeed, it is a "part of the game." I do not know anyone besides this interim coach who thinks that the "good" foul is cheating. Here we have a situation where the unwritten rules that represent the spirit of the game take precedence over the written rules. This kind of activity actually enhances the game. Clearly, part of Coach McClain's success in compiling a 7–4 record was based on his use of this heady strategy. Teaching kids to think in pressure situations is a part of the duty of a head coach and he was apparently doing this well.

Second, had the interim coach talked to Coach McClain and the principal about this specific situation, they might have convinced him of its value. If he could not come to terms with them, he should not have taken the position of interim. Indeed, not only has he not fulfilled his duty as a coach in giving his team the best chance to win the game, he has made things worse concerning the teaching of morals. Now the boys are confused as to what is good sportsmanship. They may decide that you can't play heady basketball and be a good sport.

Conclusion. I agree and disagree with the author's decision. He was right regarding the first situation and wrong regarding the second. In both situations, however, he failed in his duties as an interim coach. His Sensing perception is especially faulty. He should know empirically that there are unwritten rules of the game that everyone accepts. The "good" foul is, indeed, "a part of the game." He should keep up with the facts. His biggest liability, however, is with his Feeling judgment. By ignoring his duties to the people involved (namely, the head coach, the principal, the players), he muddies the moral waters. Because he does not take into account the role he must play as an interim, he fails to teach these boys anything about good sportsmanship. In my opinion, he did not put the boys' welfare ahead of his bias against the way the game is being played today. He tried to force them to play the way he thought it should ideally be played.

3. A dialectic with the NT functions.

What will be the consequences of the action taken to the society at large (N) if they are habitual and done consistently (T) over a long period of time?

I believe the answer to this question generally supports my point of view. First, if holding an opponent (the practice Coach McClain was teaching Brandon) was legalized it would change the game of basketball into a much more physical game. It would not be recognized as basketball. Second, the "good" foul is already habitual and done consistently. It is true, however, that some leagues have taken steps to give greater penalties for "intentional fouls." I suppose one must ask whether or not the "good" foul has changed the game into something it was not intended to be. Perhaps we must pause here for further reflection since it is true that basketball officials have detected a problem. If there was not a problem, why would they be attaching greater penalties to the "good" foul?

Revisiting the ST and SF Analyses

The ST and SF points of view are grounded in the facts of the case. STs and SFs are likely to examine rules and roles extensively in their quest to *do what's right*. If these rules are written (as in basketball) then they are likely to explore them in a highly legalistic way (especially STs). SFs may be adept at perceiving hidden or unwritten rules. STs and SFs are likely to differ on what is at stake. The ST analysis concentrates solely on the action: Is it cheating or not? The SF analysis focuses on whether the action is appropriate in that particular human circumstance: Is deliberately fouling an opponent acceptable in ninth grade basketball?

In answering the question of *how one decides,* the ST analysis uses logic in the form of universal rules and syllogisms. This is done impersonally and skillfully within the parameters outlined (a basketball contest). The SF argument focuses on the competing duties of the interim coach. This analysis gives ample weight to the care-giving responsibilities that are exercised or not exercised.

In the *dialogical step,* the ST wrestles with the future implications for the individuals involved while the SF considers the future implications for the game of basketball.

NT Justice

1. What should I do? Seek the good by considering:

(N) What is at stake? The main ethical dilemma in this case is: Is breaking the rules always cheating? This case is about outcomes of certain kinds of behavior, namely rules violations in basketball. Do these violations bring about situations that are unfair for the teams involved? Violations that produce inequality should not be condoned; violations that do not produce inequality may be accepted. Sometimes, the ends justify the means.

(N) What could happen? There are two situations that must be considered separately. First, a defensive player holds an offensive pivot skillfully so that the defensive player cannot receive a pass. The defensive player's intention is to deceive the referee and not get caught. If the defensive player is successful, he may create an unfair advantage. If, however, he gets caught in the act, no unfair advantage was created. Indeed, if he is caught five times, he will have fouled out of the game. The rules allow each player five fouls before being removed. Furthermore, the case does not specify whether or not the opposing team was employing the same strategy against Brandon's team. If the opposing team's big man was skillfully holding Brandon so that he could not receive the pass, then Coach McClain may have initiated this strategy in order to equalize things for his team. If that was not the case and if the referee was not calling the holding, then an unfair situation probably existed. Thus, in this situation it is unclear whether or not an advantage was gained because: (1) sometimes a defensive player who holds an offensive pivot gets called for a foul and (2) it is unclear whether or not the strategy was an adjustment by the coach for the inability of the referee to call a fair game.

The second situation involves the so-called "good" foul whereby a team purposefully fouls a poor free-throw shooter in hopes that he will miss and they will get the ball back. This strategy is often used at the end of games by the team that is behind. Now the question we again are looking at is: Is an unfair situation created by the actions of the players? We begin by examining the motive of the defensive team, which is behind. They want to prevent the offensive team from scoring and, furthermore, since time is running out, they want to get the ball back quickly. The defensive team may be stalling. In order to equalize this situation, they foul to stop the clock. (It should be noted that some leagues institute a shot clock to prevent stalling. Where no shot clock exists, fouling becomes the only way to equalize this situation.) Of course, it is prudent to foul the player who is least likely to make his free throws. Now what is the result of fouling in this situation? Three things can happen: the offensive player can make two free throws, or he can make one of two free throws, or he can miss them both. In my opinion, no inequality or unfairness has been brought into existence by the action of the defensive player since the offensive player is now given an opportunity to score points. If he is a poor free-throw shooter he could practice free throws and get better. Furthermore, if the team that was behind goes ahead as a result of their strategy, the team that is now behind could use the same strategy and might pull back ahead. The "good" foul does not seem to me to create a situation in basketball that is unfair. Indeed, the end result is that intrigue and tension are added to the game, making it more interesting.

2. How should I decide? Determine the just response by considering:

(T) An impersonal principle of justice. In these kinds of situations in sports and in life, the following principle should apply: The morally correct action is the one that promotes the greatest amount of good (Mill). It is our responsibility to predict to the best of our abilities which course of action we will take to produce the greatest amount of positive consequences for everyone involved. In the two situations above, I attempt to determine the outcomes of the various courses of action. Now I will specify the positives and negatives associated with each alternative based on logical analysis.

(T) **Logical syllogisms.** In the first situation, in which a defensive player holds an offensive pivot skillfully in order not to be detected by the referee, we must consider whether the outcome is positive or negative. In a basketball game, or any competitive game for that matter, the positive result is a well-played, fair competition. This is what the players, coaches, parents, and schools want. If, in the scenarios above (under section N), the deliberate and deceptive holding is being done by both teams, then the result is positive. Coach McClain would be morally right to teach his players to do this since the result is that the game is made more fair. If, however, only Coach McClain is instructing such "illegal" activity, then it would be wrong since the result is that the game is made less fair. In short, the following syllogism supports the argument above: (1) the purpose of basketball rules is to create a fair and competitive game between opponents; (2) if breaking or adjusting the rules does not create an unfair situation and enhances the competitiveness of the game, then it is morally acceptable; therefore; (3) deliberate and deceptive fouls in basketball may under certain circumstances be acceptable.

In the second situation, in which a defensive player deliberately fouls a player to put him on the free throw line, the analysis is much clearer. In the N section above, I argue that no unfair situation is created in employing the "good" foul and that, indeed, it appears to make the game more competitive and interesting. Again, are the results of the "good" foul positive or negative for all concerned? Since both teams readily employ this strategy as a "part of the game," there is no unfair situation. In fact, even if both teams did not employ the strategy, it does not create an unfair situation, in my opinion. In short, the following syllogism supports the argument above: (1) the purpose of basketball rules is to create a fair and competitive game between opponents; (2) if breaking or adjusting the rules does not create an unfair situation and enhances the competitiveness of the game, then it is morally acceptable; therefore, (3) the "good" foul is always to be considered morally acceptable in a basketball game.

Conclusion. I disagree with Coach Browne regarding his assessment of both kinds of fouls. I think he fails the intuitive test in that he does not consider the consequences of these fouls. Nor does he consider how these kinds of actions are similar to other situations in other sports. For example, the "good" foul is similar to taking a penalty stroke in golf for a bad lie, intentionally walking a good hitter in baseball, or taking a delay of game penalty in football to give the punter a better angle. These are situations where one maximizes the rules in heady play. Since they are an accepted part of the game, it does not create an unfair advantage. While Coach Browne uses logic in his analysis, I disagree with his logic. He says, "Cheating is cheating. Intentionally holding is not a part of the game of basketball. It is against the rules." If this were a syllogism it would be: (1) deliberately violating the rules of basketball is cheating; (2) holding is deliberately violating the rules; therefore; (3) holding is cheating. I do not agree with his first presupposition. Indeed, the basic question I begin with is whether deliberately violating the rules of basketball is considered cheating. And since, as I have stated, deliberately violating the rules does not necessarily create an unfair advantage, the first presupposition is false. His entire syllogism then falls apart. In conclusion, I believe that most coaches would agree with my assessment of these two kinds of fouls. I rest my case.

3. A dialectic with the SF functions.

How does the specific action taken (S) demonstrate personal faithfulness to those individuals with whom there is a relationship (F)?

On second thought, one would be wise to consider not only how the game of basketball should be played but how ninth graders are to be taught how to play. If there is a flaw in my argument, it would have to do with whether or not ninth graders are cognitively mature enough to realize that there are appropriate times to break the rules and appropriate times to follow the rules. I suppose that must be taken into account here. The question should be: At what age do you begin teaching players a gamesmanship that skirts or breaks the rules without violating the spirit of the game? I will have to reconsider my stance based on this question.

NF Compassion

1. What should I do? Seek the good by considering:

(N) What is at stake? The main ethical dilemma in this case is: Is the interim coach acting in the best interest of his players? Determining this will not be easy since we can't know his motives completely. There are, however, some hints about his motives, from his behavior and reasoning, which we will consider. The bottom line for me will be whether or not the interim coach's actions are helpful or harmful to his ninth grade boys.

(N) What could happen? The two situations described by the interim coach are completely different and must be treated separately. First, Coach McClain has taught one player on the team, Brandon, how to hold an offensive player skillfully so that he will not be detected by the referee. This is against the rules of basketball since you are not permitted to hold a player. The game-time result of such behavior, provided Brandon is not caught, is that the offensive player is unable to catch the ball. Brandon's team may force a turnover or, at least, keep the ball out of the paint. This appears to give Brandon's team an advantage through illegal means. Of course, if Brandon is caught by the referee and given a foul, there is no advantage gained. We should note that only Brandon has been taught this "illegal" skill and I would like to know why this is the case. This kind of deception is similar to some other kinds of deception sometimes taught by coaches. In football, for example, coaches will sometimes teach offensive linemen how to hold the defensive linemen so that the referee will not detect it. In hockey, coaches teach players to go down hard on the ice and try to draw a roughing penalty on the other team. This is similar to "flopping" in basketball in order to draw a charge. In each case, the intent is to deceive the referee.

In the second situation, Coach McClain (like most every other coach in the game of basketball) has taught the entire team, not just one person, that they should foul a poor free throw shooter late in the game in order to stop the clock and put that player on the line. This is a typical strategy employed at nearly every level of basketball, including recreational ball. It is similar to intentionally walking a good hitter in baseball, taking a penalty stroke in golf to improve a lie, or taking a delay of game penalty in football to improve the angle for a punter. In each case, the intent is to take full advantage of the rules so that you are placed in the best position to win. This action is very different from the first situation since the player willfully accepts the penalty. There is no intent to deceive the referee.

2. How should I decide?

(F) **Determine the most caring response.** Again, we will take each situation separately. Regarding the first one, I am inclined to believe that the interim coach has a point. Coach McClain may himself realize that this tactic is inappropriate since he has only taught it to Brandon. If he felt this kind of deception was OK, it seems that he would have taught it openly to all of his players. The main problem here is deception. Coach McClain is teaching Brandon to break the rules and get away with it. I think it is problematic to teach this to a ninth grader. Brandon is probably a fourteen or fifteen-year-old boy. He is at an impressionable age. It is sometimes said that sports build character. I believe this. Sports should teach children team work, good sportsmanship, patience, etc. Sports should not be used as an arena to teach how to deceive the authorities. We have enough problems in our society today with kids who do not respect rules or adults. We simply cannot teach our children this kind of behavior. It's not right. Furthermore, Hewitt Catholic High School is a religious school committed to teaching values. Surely the parish priest would not condone this kind of education in his parish. This does not mean, however, that I believe this kind of behavior would be unacceptable at the college or professional level of basketball. At the higher levels, where adults are playing, such behavior may be appropriate and simply "a part of the game." Now it is also possible (though we are not given such information) that Coach McClain is teaching this skill to Brandon because Brandon is being held illegally. Some would argue that if Brandon holds deceptively because he is being held deceptively then this would equalize things. While that might be true I still think the coach should not teach this to Brandon since now he is teaching him that "two wrongs make a right." Retaliation is not something we should be teaching our kids in sports. Finally, since it may be, and likely is the case that Brandon is not being illegally held, Brandon's engagement in this activity could lead to problems on the court with the opposing player. A coach should not teach behavior that is likely to result in ill-will between players. To compete in a sportsmanlike way is hard enough for fourteen-year-olds without putting more obstacles in their way. So I believe that the interim coach was acting in Brandon's best interest by stopping this activity. I'm not convinced that he put an end to it in the right way but nonetheless he did apparently put an end to it.

Regarding the second issue, I am of the opinion that the interim coach acted improperly and did not do what was in the best interest of his players. Here the situation is completely different. Does the interim coach have ulterior motives? He seems more concerned about correcting the way basketball is played than he does about his team. The team he inherited was not very talented but had played well. The interim coach seems to put his own idealistic, out-dated style of play above that of the team. This little team deserves a fighting chance. He takes it away from them. It is perhaps likely that the interim coach knows this at some level since he is unwilling to be completely honest with the principal. He does not tell the principal that he will not allow the team to commit the "good" foul. Surely, if he had done that the principal, if he knows anything about basketball, would have objected. This hyper-concern for the rules is distasteful to me. He overturns Coach McClain's coaching without considering the results of less competitive play, ambiguity of the players about what is right and wrong, and ill-will between parents and coach. This kind of idealism will backfire. The players will not learn good sportsmanship as a result. In fact, they will come to laugh at sportsmanship. While the "good" foul may not follow the letter of the law it does follow the spirit of the law and should certainly be taught at this level of basketball.

I would argue, however, that at some lower levels of basketball the "good" foul would be inappropriate. For example, in an elementary school league, fouling a poor free throw shooter and putting him in a position to lose the game could be detrimental to his fragile self-esteem. Coaches at that level must be sensitive to humiliating an opponent. So again it all depends on the situation.

Conclusion. I agree with the author regarding his assessment of the first foul but disagree regarding the second foul. I think he fails the intuitive test in that he does not consider the consequences of these fouls. Nor does he consider how these kinds of actions are similar to other situations in other sports. Coach Browne seems to base his argument on the idea that if an action is against the rules it must be wrong. While I don't buy into that argument, I do think he takes the right stand on the first kind of foul discussed. He could have bolstered his argument here by using his Feeling judgment, arguing that teaching deception is illegitimate in a Christian educational setting. Also, had he used his Feeling judgment in evaluating the second foul, he might have foreseen the negative consequences his actions would have on the boys and their parents. So, I am not particularly pleased with the way Coach Browne presents his arguments and can understand why players and parents were upset with him.

3. A dialectic with the ST functions.

Am I willing to allow for the specific action I take (S) to be made public and codified (T) for general usage?

The specific action is to stop teaching deception but to continue teaching the "good" foul. If I had argued that it was appropriate to teach deception I might be in trouble with this question since making it public and acceptable for general usage would change the game of basketball into a wrestling match. In regards to the "good" foul, I believe that such action is indeed already made public and codified for general usage. That's why everyone calls it the "good" foul. Even so, recent rule changes at various levels of basketball give additional penalties for intentional fouls (e.g., two free throws and the ball back) give me pause to consider whether the "good" foul changes the game for ill. I don't think it does but this question does cause me to reconsider.

Revisiting the NT and NF Analyses

Through their intuitive ability, NT and NF types are likely to quickly evaluate what is at stake. They are likely to determine the focus of the case without getting into the details. STs and SFs, on the other hand, want to consider all of the details before determining what is at stake. While NTs and NFs are both concerned with the results (seeking the good), their bottom-line is different. The NT analysis focuses on whether rule violations produce inequality for the teams involved. The ends justify the means. The NF analysis focuses on whether the interim coach acts in the best interest of his players. Thus, the motives of the coach become important. Once a determination has been made concerning what is at stake, NT and NF analysis proceeds to brainstorm the possibilities and scenarios involved. Intuitive types are often proficient at considering "what ifs." This wide-open exploration of the problem may lead to the discovery of analogous situations (e.g., How is the "good" foul in basketball like the intentional walk in baseball?).

In answering the question of *how one decides* the case once the primary issue is identified, NT analysis uses logic in the form of principles and syllogisms. This is done with precision and objectivity within the focused arena of exploration (basketball). NF judgment examines intentions: why do the coaches do what they do? What do they hope to bring about? This analysis gives import to the care-giving responsibilities of the participants.

In the *dialogical step,* the NT considers how the advocated action is dutiful to individuals with whom there is a relationship while the NF weighs the action if made into a universal requirement.

Conclusion

The point of these analyses is to show that there are varying ways to approach a moral dilemma. The perspectives presented above demonstrate the strengths and weaknesses of a different types' moral intelligence.

STs and SFs, with their conscience of principle, fully explore the rules and roles of a given situation in order to do what's right. The precision and clarity of the ST analysis of the rules accompanied by a consistent and universal application of the rules, presents a formidable argument based on principles. The SF analysis, though principally oriented, is different. Here, the complexity of the situation is explored beyond the written rules of basketball to the competing duties of a caregiver, the interim coach.

NTs and NFs, with their conscience of potential, look beyond the rules to the various possible outcomes as they seek the good. The NT analysis explores the consequences of various rule violations to the communities involved (in this case, the basketball teams). This is done with impartiality and with an eye for consistency and coherence. The NF analysis seeks the good result by focusing on the specific context with less concern for universal implications. Thus the need to examine the interim coach's intentions. The shift is to the immediate results of the actions as they produce actual change in individual lives.

The virtues of our dominant and auxiliary functions are also our faults. What is crucial for moral integrity is the ability to dialogue with our tertiary and inferior functions. These weaker functions provide the checks and balances we need so that our moral deliberations do not become one-sided and self-righteous. We can acknowledge our own limitations in moral decision making by consciously entering into a dialectic with our tertiary and inferior functions. This can be done by asking the questions which were posed in the case study above.

The ST asks: How is the decision going to affect (N) the people involved in this situation (F)?

The SF asks: What will be the consequences of the action taken to the society at large (N) if they are habitualized and done consistently (T) over a long period of time?

The NT asks: How does the specific action taken (S) demonstrate personal faithfulness to those individuals with whom there is a relationship (F)?

The NF asks: Am I willing to allow for the specific action I take (S) to be made public and codified (T) for general usage?

These questions force us to carry on an internal dialogue which will pay important moral dividends.

If we are fortunate enough to have a friend, spouse, or colleague who is our typological opposite, we can engage their perspectives in this same way. These special people in our lives often incarnate the moral virtues that we neglect. John Beebe writes that an opposing perspective can be both internal and external:

> What this *other* may be is problematic: it might be either another person or a value associated with the self, in fact it is almost always both. It can be felt as an objective fact of one's own being or truly as an otherness belonging to someone or something else. It is the function of integrity to remember our obligation to this other. . . . (p. 34)

Thus, our pathway to integrity while uniquely ours must engage what we do not own. This obligation to seek the other perspective even as we walk our particular moral path helps us to realize a final destination that exhibits justice and care, duty and compassion.

Chapter Seven

WE MUST OF COURSE REFRAIN FROM DOING ANYTHING AGAINST NATURE; BUT HAVING TAKEN THIS INTO CONSIDERATION, LET US FOLLOW OUR OWN NATURE; AND EVEN IF WE SHOULD FIND SOMETHING BETTER ELSEWHERE, LET US USE OUR OWN NATURE AS THE STANDARD FOR REGULATING OUR WILLS.

— CICERO

Conclusion: Integrity

The American Heritage Dictionary of the English Language defines *integrity* in the following ways:

> 1. Steadfast adherence to a strict moral or ethical code. See Synonyms at *honesty.* 2. The state of being unimpaired; soundness. 3. The quality or condition of being whole or undivided; completeness [Middle English *integrite,* from Old French, from Latin *integritas,* soundness, from *integer,* whole, complete.] (s.v. "integrity")

A Jungian perspective identifies integrity with wholeness (the third definition above). Morality and wholeness are synonymous: that is, being morally complete cannot be achieved without psychological integration. Psychological integration, or what Jung calls "individuation," is achieved, in part, through the development of all four functions of consciousness: Sensing, Intuition, Thinking, and Feeling.

In defining morality in this way, we note two basic points. First, a Jungian perspective on morality honors what is of Nature. As Cicero says, " . . let us use our own nature as the standard for regulating our wills" (*De Officiis* I, xxxi, 110). John Beebe interprets this to mean that we must " . . always seek . . . to live in accord with Nature's law [since] [t]his part of our own nature is actively interested in maintaining a continuity of Nature's intent" (p. 13). In other words, we must measure our moral undertakings against the rule of our typology. SF types must honor their natural tendency to do the right thing for others; NT types must honor their natural tendency to seek the good consistently; etc. Here, we are valuing what is sometimes called "gifts differing" or, in this particular case, consciences differing. While a culture or group may emphasize a particular way of doing ethics as superior to all others, individuals within the group may have gifts of great value that stand out as different from the norm. When we honor our nature we follow the Shakespearean rule of thumb: " . . to thine own self be true, and it must follow, . . . thou canst not then be false to any man." So the first step in having integrity is recognizing the peculiar intelligence of our morality.

Second, a Jungian perspective argues that moral integrity occurs through the dialectical contention of opposites. While Nature gifts us with particular strengths (e.g., a dominant Thinking function), Nature also wills that our weaknesses (e.g., an inferior Feeling function) be developed. The development of the weaker functions (which are opposite from and contend with the dominant functions) is essential for individuation. Unless the less conscious functions become conscious, we are likely to become one-sided and narrow. The Gnostic Gospel of Thomas 45: 29–33 reads:

> If you bring forth what is within you, what is within you
> will save you. If you do not bring forth what is within you,
> what is within you will destroy you. (NHL)

Bringing forth the weaker functions provides the dialectical contention of opposites necessary for moral integrity.

Beebe, in *Integrity in Depth*, argues that a psychological definition of integrity must be sought through a dialectic between the Thinking and Feeling functions and through the Sensing and Intuitive functions (p. 32). The consistency of Thinking contends with the compassion of Feeling; the intuitive seeking of the good contends with the sense of doing what's right. Out of this dialectic may emerge thesis, antithesis, and synthesis. The NF type who seeks the good for others (thesis), should also considers the ST perspective of doing what's right consistently (antithesis), and out of this dialectic emerges a synthesis. In this way, morality is not one-sided or narrow but allows for competing opposites to be heard.

Jungian analyst Erich Neumann wrote that "whatever leads to wholeness is 'good'; whatever leads to splitting is 'evil'" (p. 126). Such morality can be applied collectively and individually. For the good of the whole—whether it be a nation, a religion, an organization, a business, or a family—all moral intelligences should be allowed their own voice. For the good of the individual, the moral contribution of each function (S, N, T, F) must be reckoned with. Within each of us, these opposites never quite agree but always contend with each other, reproaching, checking, and inspiring the decisions we make. Knowing ourselves typologically aids our ability to make consistent and compassionate decisions based on the principles of the right and the potential for the good.

Appendix

Exercises to Explore the Pathways to Integrity

Sensing–Intuition Differences:
Conscience of Principle or Conscience of Potential

1. Have you ever had to make a decision that went against your principles but seemed to be the best for all involved? Have you ever had to make a decision based on principle but which had some negative consequences for those involved? Explain.

2. Discuss the following case, keeping in mind the consciences of principle and potential:

> Matthew, a learning disabled student in college, is a star football player. He must pass an English class during the summer before his senior year in order to be eligible for his final football season. While his GPA is so low that he will not be able to graduate before his scholarship runs out, he has an excellent chance of being drafted by an NFL team and making millions of dollars once the college season is over. But he needs to be eligible in order to play. As the summer session ends, Matthew is doing poorly in the English class and asks a tutor to write his research paper for him. Unless he gets an A, he will fail the class. The tutor writes the paper, Matthew gets an A on the paper, and barely passes the class to regain his eligibility. The head coach of the football team later finds out what happened. Should the coach report this and have Matthew declared ineligible? What is best for Matthew? What is best for the football team? What is best for the university?

3. Some studies indicate that having a student dress code in school impacts learning in a positive way. To what extent, if any, should individual expression in clothing, hair style, and body piercing be repressed for the sake of good grades?

4. Animals such as rats, mice, and monkeys have sometimes been used to test certain kinds of experimental drugs. This can and often does result in suffering and death for these animals. Can this practice be morally justified? Why or why not?

5. Some people believe that assisted suicide should be a choice for certain individuals who are terminally ill. Is it morally acceptable for physicians to help a patient to choose death prematurely? Why or why not?

6. Discuss the following case, keeping in mind the consciences of principle and potential:

> Joseph Fletcher presents the following case. "Along the Wilderness Road. . . , in the eighteenth century, westward through the Cumberland Gap to Kentucky, many families and trail parties lost their lives in border and Indian warfare. Compare two episodes in which pioneers were pursued by savages. (1) [One] woman saw that her suckling baby, ill and crying, was betraying her and her three other children, and the whole company, to the Indians. But she clung to her child, and they were caught and killed. (2) [Another] woman, seeing how her crying baby endangered another trail party, killed it with her own hands, to keep silence and reach the fort. Which woman made the right decision?" (pp. 124–125)

7. Discuss the following case, keeping in mind the consciences of principle and potential:

> In 1993, ATF agents, posing as college students, set up an undercover house across the road from the home of the Branch Davidians in Waco, Texas. One agent, Robert Rodriquez, pretending to be interested in Davidian theology, began attending Bible study sessions at Mt. Carmel. His aim was to use entrapment to catch the Davidians in illegal activity. Is this kind of deception justified? Why or why not?

8. Are your professional ethics in the work place different from your personal ethics? If so, justify why.

Thinking–Feeling Differences: The option of Justice or the option of Care

1. There are many ways we can develop our feelings of empathy for those who are different from us. We can become involved in community service, we can travel to another country, we can become friends with persons of different ethnic groups or religions, etc. In what ways, if any, has your involvement with people who are different from you affected your perspective on a particular ethical issue? Should we allow our feelings to affect our moral commitments?

2. Martin Luther King, Jr. advocated love of the oppressor as the way of social change while Malcom X argued that anger toward the oppressor was the proper attitude necessary for reform. What do you think about using the feelings of love or anger as motivating tools in the quest for a just society? Can this be effective? Can our feelings lead us to justice and equity?

3. Consider a moral opinion that you held as a child or as a youth but which you no longer hold today. Why did your opinion on this issue change when you became an adult? Was it a result of a change in your reasoning ability or a result of a life experience or a result of something else?

4. In making ethical decisions is it more important that we be consistent or compassionate? Illustrate your answer with specific examples.

Endnotes

Chapter 1

1. Note that while Jung typically uses the term "sensation," Myers and Briggs typically use the term "Sensing."

Chapter 3

1. This is what Confucians called the "rectification of names."

Chapter 4

1. It can be argued that "What should I do?" is a judgment question which needs an answer from our judging functions, either Thinking or Feeling. I suggest, however, that the answer to the question comes from our perceiving functions and is, therefore, a moral given. We answer the question of "What should I do?", not on the basis of our logical or affective reasoning, but, rather, on the basis of our particular conscience, derived from either Sensing or Intuition. Our conscience will tell us what to do.

2. We note that Hinman uses the term emotion here rather than Feeling. While Jung's theory on typology does not equate Feeling with emotion, Hinman's use of the term "emotion" points us to the Jungian perspective that we make moral judgments by affective means as well as logical means.

3. The categorization of ethical theories always risks over-generalization and falsification. The argument being expressed here is that Ross is primarily a deontologist evaluating the correctness of the concrete action (S) through the "the personal character of duty" (F). Ross opposes consequentialism as he feels that it is not consistent with how ordinary people make ethical decisions. Ethical decisions for most people are common sense judgments (SF). Yet, clearly, Ross acknowledges Intuition as an important component of ethical inquiry. The term *prima facie,* itself, is a reference to Intuition since he is saying that we know things to be intrinsically good or bad, true or false. He argues that it is self-evidently true that if I make a promise to someone that I ought to keep that promise. This is ethical intuitionism since he gives no reasons (T), no feelings (F), or rules (S) why such is the case. Yet for Ross, it is not *prima facie* or self-evident which duty takes precedence over another duty. So Ross is not an intuitionist concerning our actual duties. Our actual duties are determined by "personal character" or subjective considerations (a component of Feeling).

4. Like other ethical theories, situation ethics cannot be absolutely reduced to two functions (i.e., N and F). Situation ethics does, in fact, use the other functions (S and T) and does pay attention to duty (a deontologi-

cal requirement). Yet as Fletcher himself admits, "situation ethics is closer to teleology [N], no doubt." (p. 96) And he argues that, from a Christian perspective, selfless love or *agape* (F) has the final say in any moral determination. Thus, situation ethics gives primacy to Intuition and Feeling above Sensing and Thinking.

Chapter 5

1. Isabel Myers developed a decision making model with this in mind which was later named the "zig-zag" process by Gordon Lawrence. The zig-zag refers to a pattern in using the four functions—S, N, T, and F—in solving a problem. In this scheme, one always begins with Sensing and ends with Feeling. The model proposed in this chapter begins with the person's dominant and auxiliary functions (e.g., NF) and then constructs a dialogical relationship with the tertiary and inferior functions (e.g., ST).

2. I am indebted to Peter Tufts Richardson for the basic design of this mandala. See his "Four Spiritualities Mandala." (Richardson, p. 186)

3. A syllogism is a form of deductive reasoning consisting of a major premise, a minor premise, and a conclusion. For example: All collegiate football teams play their games on Saturday (the major premise); The Baylor Bears are a collegiate football team (minor premise); therefore, the Baylor Bears play their games on Saturday (the conclusion).

Chapter 6

1. This is a fictitious case study constructed from the moral problem posed by Warren Fraleigh (Fraleigh, "Why the Good Foul Is Not Good" in Philosophic Inquiry in Sport, pp. 267–270). Fraleigh argues that the "good" foul is unethical. Part of his logic in doing so is employed under the ST analysis.

2. The argument advanced here is consistent with Warren Fraleigh's argument in "Why the Good Foul Is Not Good."

References &
Bibliography

References

The American Heritage Dictionary of the English Language. Third edition. 1992. Boston: Houghton Mifflin Company.

Beebe, John. 1995. *Integrity in Depth.* New York: Fromm International Publishing Corporation.

Bhagavad Gita. Translated by Philip Novak in Philip Novak (Ed.) *The World's Wisdom: Sacred Texts of the World's Religions.* 1994. San Francisco: HarperSanFrancisco.

The Holy Bible. New Revised Standard Version.

Blair, Karin. 1977. *Meaning in Star Trek.* Chambersburg, PA: Anima Books.

Cicero. *De Officiis.* As rendered by Emile Brehier, translated from the French by Wade Baskin, in *The Hellenistic and Roman Age.* 1965. Chicago: University of Chicago Press.

Confucian Analects. Translated by Ezra Pound. 1993. Oxford: Oxford University Press.

Fletcher, Joseph. 1967. *Situation Ethics: The New Morality.* Philadelphia: The Westminster Press.

Fraleigh, Warren. 1988. Why the Good Foul Is Not Good. In William J. Morgan and Klaus V. Meier (Eds.), *Philosophic Inquiry in Sport,* 267–270. Champaign, IL: Human Kinetics Publishers, Inc.

The Gospel of Thomas. (The Nag Hammadi Library).

Gray, John. 1992. *Men are from Mars, Women are from Venus.* San Francisco: HarperCollins Publishers.

Hinman, Lawrence. 1994. *Ethics: A Pluralistic Approach to Moral Theory.* Ft. Worth: Harcourt Brace College Publishers.

Jackson, Phil. 1995. *Sacred Hoops: Spiritual Lessons of a Hardwood Warrior.* New York: Hyperion.

Jung, C. G. 1949. Foreword. In Erich Neumann, *Depth Psychology and a New Ethic.* (1990). Boston: Shambhala Publications, Inc.

Kant, Immanuel. 1785/1959. Translated by Lewis White Beck. *Foundations of the Metaphysics of Morals.* New York: The Bobbs-Merrill Company, Inc.

Marshall, I. N. 1968. The Four Functions: A Conceptual Analysis. *Journal of Analytical Psychology,* 13:1, 1–32.

Mill, John Stuart. 1863/1957. *Utilitarianism.* New York: The Bobbs-Merrill Company, Inc.

Myers, I. B. and M. H. McCaulley. 1985. *Manual: A Guide to the Development and Use of the Myers-Briggs Type Indicator* (2nd ed.). Palo Alto, CA: Consulting Psychologists Press, Inc.

Myers, I. B., M. H. McCaulley, N. L. Quenk & A. L. Hammer. 1998. *Manual: A Guide to the Development and Use of the Myers-Briggs Type Indicator* (3rd ed.). Palo Alto, CA: Consulting Psychologists Press, Inc.

Neumann, Erich. 1990. *Depth Psychology and a New Ethic.* Boston: Shambhala.

Noddings, Nel. 1984. *Care: A Feminine Approach to Ethics and Moral Education.* Berkeley: University of California Press.

Richardson, Peter Tufts. 1996. *Four Spiritualities.* Palo Alto, CA: Davies-Black Publishing.

Ross, W. D. 1930. *The Right and the Good.* Oxford: Clarendon Press.

Spoto, Angelo. 1995. *Jung's Typology in Perspective.* Wilmette, IL: Chiron Publications.

Stein, Murray. 1993. *Solar Conscience/Lunar Conscience: An Essay on the Psychological Foundations of Morality, Lawfulness, and the Sense of Justice.* Wilmette, IL: Chiron Publications.

Tao-te Ching. Translated by D. C. Lau 1963. London: Penguin Books.

Bibliography

Ethics and Jungian Psychology

Beebe, John. 1995. *Integrity in Depth.* New York: Fromm International Publishing Corporation.

Lewis, Hunter. 1990. *A Question of Values.* San Francisco: Harper and Row. Note: This book, though not based on Jungian psychology, highlights the moral dimensions of logic, emotion, sensing, and intuition.

Neumann, Erich. 1990. *Depth Psychology and a New Ethic.* Boston: Shambhala.

Stein, Murray. 1993. *Solar Conscience/Lunar Conscience: An Essay on the Psychological Foundations of Morality, Lawfulness, and the Sense of Justice.* Wilmette, IL: Chiron Publications.

Primary Readings in Ethical Theory

Gilligan, Carol. 1982. *In a Different Voice.* Cambridge: Harvard University Press.

Kant, Immanuel. 1785/1959. Translated by Lewis White Beck. *Foundations of the Metaphysics of Morals.* New York: The Bobbs-Merrill Company, Inc.

Kohlberg, Lawrence. 1981 and 1984. *Essays in Moral Development.* New York: Harper & Row.

Fletcher, Joseph. 1967. *Situation Ethics: The New Morality.* Philadelphia: The Westminster Press.

Mill, John Stuart. 1863/1957. *Utilitarianism.* New York: The Bobbs-Merrill Company, Inc.

Ross, W. D. 1930. *The Right and the Good.* Oxford: Clarendon Press.

Typology

Jung, C. G. 1971. *Psychological Types.* Vol. 6 of *The Collected Works of C. G. Jung.* Princeton, NJ: Princeton University Press.

Lawrence, Gordon. 1993. *People Types and Tiger Stripes.* Gainesville, FL: Center for Applications of Psychological Type, Inc.

Myers, I. B., M. H. McCaulley, N. L. Quenk & A. L. Hammer. 1998. *Manual: A Guide to the Development and Use of the Myers-Briggs Type Indicator* (3rd ed.). Palo Alto, CA: Consulting Psychologists Press, Inc.

Spoto, Angelo. 1995. *Jung's Typology in Perspective.* Wilmette, IL: Chiron Publications.

Wilmer, Harry A. 1987. *Practical Jung: Nuts and Bolts of Jungian Psychotherapy.* Wilmette, IL: Chiron Publications.

_____. 1994. *Understandable Jung: The Personal Side of Jungian Psychology.* Wilmette, IL: Chiron Publications.

Group Exercises for Type Differentiation

Fields, Margaret U. and Jean B. Reid. 1999. *Shape Up Your Program: Tips,*

OTHER BOOKS OF INTEREST

FATHER, SON, AND HEALING GHOSTS
By Anthony Moore

Follow the journey of Anthony Moore in his search to learn about his father and therefore himself. Moore opens a door through time that recounts the fear and comradery of World War II discovering the father who died at twenty-three years old shortly after Anthony was born. Employing rich Jungian philosophy, Father, Son, and Healing Ghost illuminates those journeys many of us take toward finding ourselves and rediscovering or reinventing our purpose in midlife.

111 pages. Paperback. Product No. 60176. $14.95

BUILDING PEOPLE, BUILDING PROGRAMS:
A PRACTITIONER'S GUIDE FOR INTRODUCING THE MBTI® TO INDIVIDUALS AND ORGANIZATIONS
By Gordon Lawrence and Charles Martin

An important tool for the practitioner who wishes to expand his or her knowledge and use of the Myers-Briggs Type Indicator® instrument. This well-crafted book offers practitioners a comprehensive guide as a supplement to the MBTI® Manual. Includes exercises for and practical uses of the Indicator, discussions on ethical pitfalls, how to select appropriate forms to fit client needs, and a general refresher course on scoring. An indispensable book for those involved in the use and teaching of the MBTI® instrument.

274 pages. Paperback. Product No.60177. $39.95

For more information about other CAPT books, products, and training seminars, call for a catalog or visit our website at **www.capt.org**

The Center for Applications of Psychological Type (CAPT) is a nonprofit organization that promotes the accurate understanding, measurement, ethical use, and practical applications of the Myers-Briggs Type Indicator® instrument. CAPT publishes and distributes books about the MBTI® instrument and its applications, produces materials and products for administration; and offers workshops and training programs for qualification and advanced education in administering the Indicator.

2815 NW 13th Street Suite 401 ▪ Gainesville FL 32609
800.723.6284